INSIGHT COMPACT GUIDE

Bali

CW01597804

Compact Guide: Bali is the ultimate quick-reference guide to this fascinating destination. It tells you all you need to know about the island's attractions, from its temples and shrines to its beautiful beaches, not forgetting its rich musical and dramatic cultures and its welcoming people.

This is one of 130 Compact Guides, combining the interests and enthusiasms of two of the world's best known information providers: Insight Guides, whose titles have set the standard for visual travel guides since 1970, and Discovery Channel, the world's premier source of nonfiction television programming.

Discovery CHANNEL

APA PUBLICATIONS
Part of the Langenscheidt Publishing Group

Insight Compact Guide: Bali

Written by: Elke Homburg and Thomas Staender
English version by: Jane Michael
Updated by: Debe Campbell
Edited by: Francis Dorai
Photography and cover picture by: Jack Hollingsworth/Apa
Design: Graham Mitchener and Maria Lord
Picture Editor: Hilary Genin
Maps: Polyglott

Editorial Director: Brian Bell
Managing Editor: Tony Halliday

CONTACTING THE EDITORS: As every effort is made to provide accurate information in this publication, we would appreciate it if readers would call our attention to any errors and omissions by contacting:
Apa Publications, PO Box 7910, London SE1 1WE, England.
Fax: (44 20) 7403 0290
e-mail: insight@apaguide.demon.co.uk

First Edition 1996
Second Edition 2002
Printed in Singapore by Insight Print Services (Pte) Ltd
Original edition © Polyglott-Verlag Dr Bolte KG, Munich

Worldwide distribution enquiries:
APA Publications GmbH & Co. Verlag KG (Singapore Branch)
38 Joo Koon Road, Singapore 628990
Tel: (65) 865 1600, fax: (65) 861 6438

Distributed in the UK & Ireland by:
GeoCenter International Ltd
The Viables Centre, Harrow Way, Basingstoke,
Hampshire RG22 4BJ
Tel: (44 1256) 817 987, fax: (44 1256) 817 988

Distributed in the United States by:
Langenscheidt Publishers, Inc.
46–35 54th Road, Maspeth, NY 11378
Tel: (1 718) 784 0055, fax: (1 718) 784 0640

www.insightguides.com

Bali

Introduction

Places

Culture

Travel Tips

△ **Pura Besakih (p61)**
The 'Mother Temple', Bali's most scared shrine.

▽ **Ayung River (p35)**
Top white-water rafting with 20 class II–IV rapids.

▷ **Neka Museum (p36)**
A superb collection that is a great introduction to all styles of Balinese painting.

▽ **Barong Dance (p49)**
This wonderful ritual dance is performed each morning at the temple in the village of Batubulan.

◁ **Pura Taman Ayun (p43)** One of Bali's most sacred, and architecturally harmonious, temples. The morning ceremony here exudes an air of peaceful calm and contemplation.

△ **Kuta/Legian (p29)** Bali's finest, and most popular, beaches – an arc of white sand and blue sea.

△ **Pura Tanah Lot (p47)** This spectacular temple, perched above the sea, is very beautiful at sunset.

◁ **Tenganan (p69)** The culture of Old Bali has been preserved in this village, famous for its books, fabrics and festivals.

△ **Rice Terraces (p72)** The terracing between Candidasa and Amlapura is one of the wonders of Bali.

◁ **Pura Gunung Kawi (p53)** The origin of these sacred monolithic reliefs, set in a picturesque valley, continues to baffle experts.

Island of Gods and Demons

Rangda and Barong, the Balinese personifications of black and white magic, pit their individual strengths against each other. It is a desperate struggle, where each is fighting to gain the upper hand. And yet, the Balinese know that neither will win. The ancient rivalry represented in this drama is more than just a competition or an absorbing form of entertainment. It represents a microcosm of the world at large where good maintains a shaky equilibrium with evil, each striving to outdo the other.

Many visitors arrive with the notion that on Bali they will find one of the world's last paradises. Intoxicated by the lilting sounds of a gamelan orchestra and the heady scent of incense sticks, a good number are lulled into believing that they have. It is an image which survives, despite the reality of Kuta with its sun-worshippers, importunate traders, marauding massage women, fast-food restaurants and ear-splitting discotheques.

Opposite: a mask representing Rangda
Below: tourist at Pura Penataran Sasih Temple
Bottom: outrigger at Sanur

Ties That Bind

With hordes of people visiting the 'Island of the Gods' every year, one might ask how long will it be before the rice farmers stop placing their faith in the power of Dewi Sri, the goddess of the rice harvest, and sell the fields for tourist development, which is already rampant on the island. Like many traditional economies the world over, Bali has opened its doors to Western culture and walks a tightrope between modernity and tradition.

Today, the struggle between Barong and Rangda, a traditional Balinese dance pitching the forces of good against evil, still ends in a draw, and the island's gods, demons and its rich cultural legacy exist alongside high technology and mass tourism. For the moment at least, the Balinese cosmos is still in harmony.

An elaborate purification ceremony takes place on the beaches each year, cleansing the island of the year's misdeeds and asking for blessings and good fortune for the Balinese. Even the presence of hundreds of gawking, camera-clicking tourists

Wallace Line
In the 19th century, the geographer-scientist Alfred Wallace established that there were marked differences in both the vegetation and animal life between Bali and the island of Lombok, which lies to the east. The large mammals of western Indonesia, from tiger and rhinoceros to elephants, gave way to marsupials and a number of bird species which were otherwise found in Australia. From this, Wallace concluded that, 100 million years ago, the Strait of Lombok represented the dividing line between the Asian and Australian continents. The division is known to this day as the Wallace Line.

Sailing in blue waters

cannot defile this ancient cathartic ritual. And it is all too easy to believe that the power of the gods will prevail over that of mere mortals, at least in the coming year.

LOCATION

Bali is the westernmost island in the chain that makes up the Lesser Sundas group. It covers 5,600sq km (2,162sq miles), making it one of the smallest provinces of the Indonesian archipelago, the largest in the world. Indonesia's 17,508 islands stretch from the Pacific to the Indian Ocean, lying on both sides of the Equator between the Malay Peninsula and New Guinea. Lying 8° south of the Equator and 115° east of Greenwich,

Bali is separated to the west from neighbouring Java by a narrow strip of sea. The Strait of Lombok, which divides Bali from the island of Lombok to the east *(see panel)* is not only considerably wider (30km/19 miles) but also much deeper.

LANDSCAPE

A chain of volcanoes runs through the islands of Sumatra and Java and continues into Bali, forming Gunung Agung (3,142m/10,308ft), the island's highest mountain, and Gunung Batur (1,717m/5,633ft). The islanders believe these volcanoes to be the abode of the gods, who in their taciturn manner, bless the island with mineral-rich volcanic ash for bountiful harvests yet remain a permanent threat. The last major eruption of Gunung Agung occurred as recently as 1963 – after lying dormant for nearly 120 years – purportedly caused by the gods who were angry.

Also of volcanic origin are the mountain lakes, of which the largest are Danau Batur and Danau Bratan found in the north of Bali. These mountain lakes feed the rivers which flow through central and southern Bali, and provide the water for the irrigation of rice fields.

DIFFERENT TERRAINS

Despite its size, Bali offers an astonishing variety of landscapes. The southern part, the most fertile region, is characterised by luxuriant tropical vegetation. In the centre lie the misty cloud-covered highlands. The emerald green rice terraces found in the south-central region are irrigated by the waters from mountain lakes and rivers. The Bukit Badung peninsula in the extreme south, on the other hand, is very arid. The northern beaches are formed out of black lava, while the east is largely covered with impenetrable jungle. The west coast, by contrast, is mainly dry and inhospitable.

Below: Sanur beach
Bottom: Lakes Buyan and Tambligan

CLIMATE AND WHEN TO GO

Bali's climate is determined by the monsoon winds and consists of two seasons. During the wet season, between November and March, the northwest monsoon brings rain and humidity which can be as high as 95 percent. The dry season from April until October is the most pleasant time to visit.

Since the island lies virtually on the Equator, daytime temperatures climb to about 30°C (86°F) almost every day, although the mountains tend to be about 10°C (18°F) cooler and may even seem chilly at night. The Northern Hemisphere summer months are definitely the best time to visit Bali, which explains why July and August are high

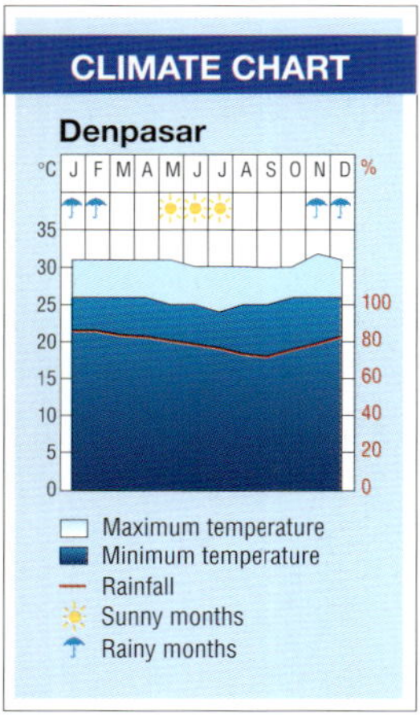

season on the island. Fewer tourists arrive during the European winter, except for Christmas, which is the summer holiday season for Australians. During these months bring along an umbrella – although a day of continuous rain is rare, several wet days at a stretch can sometimes occur.

NATURE AND ENVIRONMENT

Rice farming is an important activity, and the countryside is characterised by a series of artistically laid-out rice terraces *(sawah)*. When ripe, the golden yellow ears sway in the breeze, caressed by Dewi Sri, the Balinese goddess of fertility, whose shrines, laden with offerings, are found in a corner of every field. Side by side with the dry fields ready for harvest are freshly flooded emerald green paddies containing young seedlings, and just around the next corner you may come across a farmer ploughing the land with the help of oxen. Bali's countryside is largely determined by its year-round rice-farming culture.

Below: rice cultivation
Bottom: ploughing time

HARVESTING RICE

Depending on the variety of rice grown, a period of three to six months will elapse between sowing and harvesting. The seedlings take root initially in seed beds before being

transplanted into the irrigated fields, where they are kept immersed in water during the entire growth period until the rice is ready for harvesting. The water from streams and rivers is diverted to the fields via channels cut into the soft volcanic rock. Thanks to Bali's fertile soil and an irrigation system perfected over centuries, a Balinese farmer can harvest two to three crops a year.

A co-operative *(subak)* ensures that the water is fairly distributed to the fields and that the dams are properly maintained. Shortly before harvest time, the fields are drained and the women of the neighbourhood gather to cut the rice using a small knife called *ani-ani*, hiding the blade in their hands in order not to frighten Dewi Sri. Today, this traditional method of harvesting is used only for Balinese rice and not for other higher-yield varieties.

Other important crops include coconuts, coffee, peanuts, spices such as cloves, cinnamon and vanilla, and tropical fruits such as bananas, pineapples, papayas and mangoes, as well as vegetables. The local wine *(anggur)* production in the north of the island is booming despite the uneven quality of the grapes produced.

FLORA AND FAUNA

Bali has been compared to a tropical garden because of the wide variety of plants which flourish there. There are various species of palm tree, bamboo groves, and flowering shrubs like hibiscus, poinsettia, bougainvillea and a profusion of orchids. The focal point of most villages is the banyan tree *(ficus benghalenis)*, with its strange aerial roots. The dry Bukit Badung peninsula is also home to the pandanus (screw-pine) and even cacti. Mangrove swamps fringe the coast between Sanur and Nusa Dua and throughout the northwest. Tropical rainforests, which once covered the entire island, are still to be found in the east.

Until a few decades ago, you could find the island's last remaining tigers, rhinoceroses and crocodiles within Bali Barat National Park, Bali's 'Wild West'. The park covers an area of 700sq km (270sq miles) and is a paradise for ornithologists.

Womanly rice
The rice cycle relies as much on religious management as on nature and secular concerns. Growing rice is regarded as the personification of Dewi Sri, the goddess of fertility, who is also manifestation of the one supreme god, known as Sanghyang Widi Wasa. Throughout the growing cycle, offerings must be made to Dewi Sri, and when the grain appears on the stalks, the rice is described as being pregnant.

Below: pineapples off to market
Bottom: floral display

Balinese plonk
Rice and palm wines have long been a staple in Bali. But grapes grown along the north coast have turned into a new domestic product – Balinese wine. Two home-grown companies produce red, rosé, white and sparkling wines from Bali's Alphonse Lavallee grapes, thought to have arrived on the island with Portuguese traders.

With luck and patience, visitors to the park will be able to see several species of birds, deer and monkey as well as the endangered wild Javan buffalo *(Bos javanicus)*.

Of the large mammal species once found on Bali, only the wild boar and deer remain. Monkeys are common, and some forests, such as Alas Kedaton, are inhabited by colonies of macaques. Lizards are also found everywhere, including the insect-eating geckos which serve a useful function in many hotel rooms. Snakes, too, are commonplace. The most important domestic animals are the sway-back pig and the pretty doe-faced Balinese cow, as well as chickens and ducks.

POPULATION

A Balinese family group

Bali's present population of some 3.125 million inhabitants trace their ancestry to the various ethnic groups which migrated to the island from southern China between 2500 and 1500BC. The population density of 558 inhabitants per sq km (1,445 per sq mile) is much greater than that, say, of the United Kingdom (232 inhabitants per sq km). The capital and largest city, Denpasar, has a population of 552,785, with more than 32 percent of the population still living in the rural areas. Bali's annual population growth rate is 1.48 percent and average life expectancy is 64 years.

THE HINDU–DHARMA RELIGION

'Life is Religion, and Religion is Life' – it is no accident that Bali is known as the 'Island of Gods and Demons'. Religion permeates every aspect of everyday life. The daily offerings of food to ancestors and spirits, a cock fight at a temple festival or the graceful dance of a young girl are all expressions of a deep religious conviction. The fascination of Balinese culture lies not least in the colourful and sensuous rituals through which the gods are worshipped.

Bali and West Lombok together form an enclave of Hinduism in the midst of the largest Muslim country in the world. But the Balinese version of the religion is very different from that practised on the Indian subcontinent.

Hinduism and Buddhism were introduced to Indonesia via Java by traders between the 8th and 16th centuries. The Javanese in turn adopted elements of both religions, and incorporated them with indigenous religious practices of their own. This peculiar form of Javanese Hinduism arrived in Bali during the 10th century when a Javanese princess married a Balinese king. During the 16th century, when the threat of a Muslim invasion became imminent in Java, the nobles of the Majapahit kingdom, the last great Hindu dynasty on Java, sought refuge on Bali.

A Hybrid Faith

Over time, this hybrid Hindu faith developed further, incorporating ancient animist beliefs in spirits and the practice of the ancestor cult handed down through the generations. Today, 94 percent of the population follows this belief, known as Hindu-Dharma or Agama Hindu.

Paying honour to ancestors, deities, spirits and demons can be traced back to pre-Hindu times, as can exorcist practices such as trance dances and sacrifices to appease bad spirits. Equally ancient is the Balinese study of cosmology, an understanding of which is essential to any comprehension

Below: Gunung Kawi
Bottom: Legong dancers

Demons and devils
Life for the Balinese would be paradise on earth if they were simply under the protection of their gods and ancestors. However, they have to contend with the powers of darkness, who rule on moonless nights. The land is haunted, in particular, by the *leyaks* and *buta kala*, the disembodied souls of the dead, who during their lifetime followed the principles of black magic, and who are likely to play tricks on the living if they are not adequately appeased.

Below: Hindu guardian deity
Bottom: temple offerings

of the Hindu-Dharma religion. The countless daily rituals that the Balinese observe mostly serve to ensure that human existence is in harmony with the cosmos and its divine principles.

The Balinese perceive their island as a macrocosm in which the mountains and space above represent *kaja*, the realm of the gods, while the earth and the space beneath, i.e. the sea, represent *kelod*, the home of the dark powers. The holy mountain Gunung Agung is the residence of the god Shiva and is regarded as the centre of the universe. Man lives in the middle kingdom between these two extremes, and the roads linking the villages, farmsteads and family temples are all aligned along an imaginary axis between the mountain and the sea. *Kaja* and *kelod*, however, also represent in general the contradictory nature of all beings. Heaven and earth, sun and moon, life and death stand in opposition to each other, for the one cannot exist without the other.

REINCARNATION

The Balinese have adopted the Hindu belief that every human being is subject to the cycle of reincarnation. For pious Hindus, much worse than death itself is the fact that they must live through an infinite number of existences until they are released. In contrast to Indian Hindus,

the Balinese believe that they will be reincarnated within their own clan. The level of reincarnation is determined by *karma pala*, the sum of all good and evil deeds which go to make up a life. A Hindu's goal is to be liberated from the cycle of reincarnation by living as virtuous a life as possible. Thus, the individual immortal soul will be united with the highest divine principle *(nirwana)*.

Apart from the Indian social order and their philosophy, the Indian traders also brought with them their mythology, including their pantheon of gods, as well as the two epics, the *Ramayana* and the *Mahabharata*. These provide the themes for shadow plays and various dance dramas.

Below: Brahma Vihara Monastery
Bottom: the Buddha is part of the Hindu pantheon

A Pantheon of Gods

The triumvirate of the highest Hindu deities (*trimurti* or *trisakti*) consists of Brahma, the creator, Wisnu, the preserver, and Shiva, the destroyer and renewer. In temples you will often notice their symbolic colours (red for Brahma, black for Wisnu and white for Shiva). Dewi Sri, the guardian of fertility in general and of rice farming in particular, and Dewi Lakshmi, responsible for happiness and prosperity, are the wives of Wisnu. Dewi Saraswati, Brahma's wife, is greatly revered as the goddess of wisdom and literature.

Finally, Shiva's consort Parvati appears in various manifestations – as Durga, the goddess of death, as well as Uma, the goddess of love. In addition, there is an almost infinite list of other deities. All gods, however, are but manifestations of one and the same god – Sanghyang Widi Wasa, the divine principle. This is in keeping with the Indonesian policy of Pancasila (Five Principles), one of which recognises the belief in one god.

For a long time, as in India, its country of origin, Buddhism was also an important religious element. In Bali today, Buddha has acquired the position of a minor Hindu deity, a protective spirit guarding the home. Some priests, however, continue to follow his teachings. They describe themselves as *pedanda boda,* as opposed to the *pedanda shiva* priests who serve the Hindu god.

Sacred offerings
Since the world of man lies between the cosmic poles, it is the duty of the Balinese to preserve the harmony. And so they worship gods and demons in equal measure, as can be seen from the small offerings called *banten*, a small palm leaf tray of flowers and rice and sprinkled with holy water. Balinese women prepare these each day with painstaking attention to detail. They are offered to the sacred ancestors in the family temple, to the demons which inhabit the doorstep or at dangerous road intersections, or to the goddess of the rice harvest, Dewi Sri, at the little shrines in the rice fields.

SACRIFICE AND PURIFICATION

Religious life on the island centres on sacrifices and purification ceremonies. Offerings consist of anything from a grain of rice to elaborately decorative food. Animals are sacrificed during a temple festival, and they may be provided by any faithful member of the community. Purification ceremonies, on the other hand, can only take place with the assistance of a priest. He serves as an intermediary between man and the gods.

The greatest respect is reserved for the *pedanda*, or high priest, a member of the Brahman caste *(see below)*. He sanctifies water for rituals, supervises important ceremonies and spends his time meditating and studying religious texts and rituals. The daily duties in the temple, on the other hand – supervising temple festivals, distributing holy water and directing processions – is the task of the *pemangku*, the assistant priest. This job is not linked to any particular caste.

A Hindu priest

THE CASTE SYSTEM AND COMMUNITY

The spread of the Hindu religion at the beginning of the 16th century was resisted by the Bali Aga, the original pre-Hindu inhabitants of the island, who still live in a handful of remote villages *(see Tenganan, page 69)*. The Hindu caste system was introduced by the Javanese Majapahit kingdom who invaded Bali in the 16th century. There are four castes, each associated with a title which indicates the caste the individual belongs to.

Brahmana, or priests, form the top caste in Balinese society. Members of this caste are known as Ida Bagu (man) and Ida Ayu (woman). The next caste, the *ksatria*, comprises the high nobility who once ruled the island, and are distinguished by titles like Anak Agung, Dewa and Cokorde. The *wesia*, who form the lower nobility, go by the title of Gusti. Only 3 percent of all Balinese belong to one of these castes, which together are known as *triwangsa*. Most Balinese are *sudra* or *jaba*, literally the outsiders of the court. Unlike India, there are no lower caste untouchables on the island.

A BALINESE HOME

The family, particularly the extended family, forms the basis of social life. In Indonesia, as in many other southeast Asian countries, it replaces the national network of social security and retirement pensions found in Western countries. The interests of the family as a whole take precedence over the rights of the individual.

A typical family home is laid out according to the rules of *kelod-kaja* *(see page 14)*, with the sleeping and living areas on the mountain side and the work rooms facing towards the sea. The complex is closed off from prying eyes by a wall, with a small free-standing wall just behind the entrance to prevent demons getting in. The individual buildings and *bale* (open pavilions) are grouped around the inner courtyard. One of these is the family pavilion in which rites of passage *(see page 99)* are celebrated. Holding pride of place are the shrines of the family and ancestors, the scene of daily prayers and offerings.

Below and bottom: village life

THE VILLAGE COMMUNITY

Despite the influence of media and tourism, the lifestyle of the younger generation of Balinese is still governed to a remarkable degree by the traditions which form the basis for family and village life. Most people are still employed in farming,

and the importance of agriculture can be seen in the predominantly rural-based social structures which prevail on the island to this day.

About 82 percent of the population live in a village community, comprising individual village units known as the *banjar*. The *banjar* determines to a large extent how village life functions and its success is due, in part, to the strong Balinese sense of community. All adult male family members, who are members of this council, decide on matters of local importance, from minor road repairs to matters such as land rent, the preparation of temple festivals and the maintenance or construction of new temples. The *banjar* also functions as an informal local court.

What's in a name?
Balinese often are named in the order of their birth: Wayan or Putu for the first born, Made for the second, Nyoman the third, and Ketut the fourth. The cyclical order begins again with the fifth child. Thus, a family may have several members with the same name.

Below and bottom: stages of rice production

RICE CO-OPERATIVES

The influence of the *banjar* is amply demonstrated in the *subak* (rice co-operative), an association of rice farmers who co-ordinate the essential tasks relating to the irrigation of the rice fields. The *subak* is also responsible for deciding when the fields should be flooded, for the division of work amongst farmers who share a common irrigation channel, and deciding when harvesting begins. In addition, it also determines the appropriate offerings to the rice goddess Dewi Sri in the *subak* temples, without whom no harvest can be successful.

LANGUAGE

Bahasa Indonesia is the official language, spoken by more than 350 ethnic groups scattered across the geographically and culturally diverse region covered by the Indonesian archipelago. Although Bahasa Indonesia is the working language in schools and the civil service in Bali and is widely spoken, the mother tongue of the people is Balinese. This is in turn divided into two versions: High Balinese and Low Balinese.

As Bahasa Indonesia not a difficult language, it is well worth trying to learn a little of the language. The grammar is easy, as Bahasa Indonesia does not distinguish between gender, nor do its verbs have tenses. Plurals are easily formed, and the rules governing word order within the sentence are flexible. The following is a brief guide to pronunciation of Bahasa Indonesia:

- **c** mostly 'ch', e.g. *candi* ('chandi', temple)
- **j** as in English 'j', e.g. *jalan* ('jalan', street)
- **y** as 'ya', e.g. *saya* ('saya', I)
- **r** 'r' is rolled
- **s** as 'ss'
- **h** final 'h' at the end of a syllable is pronounced with an audible expiration of air.
- **e** is usually pronounced 'ay', e.g. *besok* ('baysok', tomorrow) or swallowed between two consonants, e.g. *berapa* ('brapa', how much).

Below: the journey to work
Bottom: plantains

ECONOMY

Over 75 percent of Bali's population is involved in agriculture. Rice is by far the most important crop, most of it grown for home consumption. In the cooler mountain regions coffee is also grown, as are cloves, fruit, vegetables, maize and coconut palms. Copra, the white flesh of the coconut, is an important export commodity. Fishing and salt extraction have been practised for many years. A new addition is the farming of shellfish in saltwater basins along the coast.

Tourism has long been the principal source of foreign exchange. Many rice farmers add to their income by letting rooms to tourists, or by producing or selling souvenirs. The island's only industry of note is clothing manufacture. Clothes are mostly created to suit Western tastes by designers from industrialised countries, sewn by Balinese women – often as a cottage industry – and sold on the island or exported.

Tourism Boom

During the 1930s, no more than 100 foreigners would arrive on Bali in a month. During the late 1960s and the 1970s, the island was regarded by hippies as the last remaining paradise on earth. Today, mass tourism is essential to the economy. Since the end of the 1980s, Bali has enjoyed a tourist boom and the expansion of hotel accommodation, which totals 40,000 rooms, seems set to continue. The number of holiday-makers has reached 1½ million a year.

Bali has long been open to Western influence, and the dichotomy between the traditional and modern worlds is very much in evidence. Work in the rice fields, formerly taken for granted, is becoming less important as tourism becomes an increasingly attractive prospect. More tourists may create more jobs, but it also reduces the Balinese attachment to other sources of income which are of immense traditional importance. The extent of the tourist industry is logical and

Below: batik salesman
Bottom: ceremonial flags on Nusa Dua beach

yet deeply questionable, bearing in mind the economic dependence it creates.

POLITICS AND ADMINISTRATION

According to its constitution, Indonesia is a centrally governed presidential republic based on the national doctrine *pancasila*, the five *(panca)* principles which have been declared the pillars *(sila)* of the state. These principles are the belief in a single all-powerful God, together with humanity, national unity, democracy and social equality. The national motto, intended to hold together the multiplicity of peoples that make up the nation, is taken from a Javan epic: *Bhinneka Tunggal Ika* (Unity in Diversity).

Indonesia is divided into 36 provinces, of which Bali is one. The province of Bali is subdivided into eight regions *(kabupaten)*, each with a capital: Badung (Denpasar), Bangli (Bangli), Buleleng (Singajara), Gianyar (Gianyar), Jembrana (Negara), Karangasem (Amlapura), Klungkung (Semarapura) and Tabanan (Tabanan). Since 2001, Bali's government has been autonomous, contributing only about 20 percent of its wealth in taxes to the central government.

TUMULTUOUS FUTURE

Indonesia has been struggling toward democracy since the fall of dictatorial President Suharto in 1998. Suharto's predecessor, President Sukarno, coined the phrase 'guided democracy' where power was concentrated in the hands of the president who ruled in an authoritarian manner. In a startling turn of events in 1998, caused by the Asian economic crisis, Suharto was overthrown amid massive street protests.

In the post-Suharto years, the country is riven by both a weak enonomy and political infighting as well as the rise of separatist movements in certain Indonesian provinces. With East Timor gaining independence in 1999, other regions like Aceh and West Papua (formerly Irian Jaya) are seeking either autonomous rule or outright independence.

Tourist economy
Tourism touches an estimated 85 percent of all Balinese economically. Whether directly working within hotels, restaurants, handicrafts, wood carving, tour guiding, or selling postcards, most Balinese earn some or all of their income from tourism.

Bottom: flying the flag

HISTORICAL HIGHLIGHTS

2500–1500 BC First wave of migrants arrive in Indonesia from south China.

1500BC The first megalithic monuments are found in Indonesia.

500BC Bronze Age culture on Bali.

AD500 Buddhism infiltrates the island.

AD1000 Dharmawanga, an east Javanese king, assumes power over Bali. Erlangga, a Balinese prince, becomes king in east Java, influencing culture in Bali. The *Ramayana* and *Mahabharata* are translated into old Javanese (Kawi) script. Bali becomes independent.

1100 'Mother Temple' Besakih is built.

End of 13th century Majapahit dynasty gains power on Java. The Pejeng dynasty rules on Bali.

15th century Islam reaches Java and precipitates fall of Majapahit dynasty. The elite flee to Bali, where the son of the last ruler is proclaimed *raja* (king) of Bali in Gelgel. Starts the Gelgel dynasty and assumes the title *Dewa Agung*, sowing the seeds of Balinese culture and religion.

Early 16th century A unified Bali conquers territories in east Java and Lombok. The first Europeans arrive in Southeast Asia. Portugal and Spain's main interest lies in the spices in Moluccas. In the second half of the century they are followed by the Dutch, who land on Bali in 1597. In 1602 the Dutch East India Company is founded to exploit Indonesia.

17th century Batavia is founded by the Dutch. The decline of the Dewa Agung allows principalities to assert independence, and autonomous Hindu kingdoms are created. Dewa Agung remains the highest-ranking *raja* on Bali. For religious reasons, the seat of government is moved to Klungkung.

17th–18th centuries The Raja of Karangasem becomes the most powerful ruler and gains control of Lombok. Bali is divided by continual feuds.

1799 The Dutch East India Company goes bankrupt and the Netherlands government takes over its administration; Indonesia becomes a colony.

1846 Dutch military expedition lands in Baleng (North Bali) where Dutch rule is established. Slavery becomes illegal and *suttee*, the self-immolation by widows in the cremation fires of their husbands, is banned.

1900 The Raja of Gianyar seeks colonial protection from the other principalities who continue internecine feuds instead of forming an alliance against the Dutch.

1904 Dutch attempts to colonise the island by force from their base in Singaraja meets with violent opposition from rajas of South Bali. When a trading ship runs aground near Sanur in 1904, the locals plunder the wreckage. The Dutch demand compensation from Raja Agung Made of Badung on behalf of the ship's owners but are refused.

1906 Negotiations fall through and the colonial government uses the incident as an excuse to declare war. A violent Dutch attack ends in ritual suicide *(puputan)* in Badung. An army of colonial troops march to the palace, but the Balinese, dressed in white, march forth to meet certain death at the hands of the Dutch. 2,000 Balinese die, including women and children. Those who are not hit by Dutch bullets draw their *keris* and kill their wounded friends, wives and children to spare them shame of capture.

1908 A similar *puputan* against foreign rule takes place in Klungkung and the battle of Marga. The island falls into Dutch hands.

1920–40 A growing Indonesian nationalist movement is repressed by the Dutch. The colonial government decides to 'protect and preserve' Bali from outside influences and exploitation. An artistic and cultural revival is inspired by visiting foreign artists and writers, anthropologists and musicologists.

1942 The Japanese invade Indonesia and remain until 1945. To win local support, they give the principal nationalist leader, General Sukarno (1901–70), considerable political latitude.

17 August 1945 Sukarno proclaims the independence of Indonesia and becomes the first president. The Dutch return and for four years there is extensive fighting between the occupying forces and guerrilla groups. Bali is pro-Dutch.

20 November 1946 In Battle of Marga in Central Bali *(see page 45)*, national hero I Gusti Ngurah Rai and 94 patriots are killed fighting against the Dutch.

1949 The Dutch confirm the Republic of Indonesia under President Sukarno, with Bali a province. Economic difficulties drive the new state into bankruptcy. Sukarno abandons his Western alliances and withdraws into political isolation.

1963 The volcano Gunung Agung erupts. Thousands are killed on Bali, and many temples and villages destroyed.

1965 A coup attempt by Indonesia's communist party made against Sukarno. The coup is surpressed and a wave of communist reprisals follow. Bali is not spared the bloodshed and between 100,000 and 200,000 people are executed.

1968 General Suharto is elected President of Indonesia, and is re-elected in 1973, 1978, 1983, 1988, 1993 and 1998. His New Order helps the national economy prosper, and direct investment and loans from the West are encouraged, but democracy is far from being achieved.

1970 The growth in mass tourism begins, transforming Bali from a hippy haven into a resort island.

1975 Indonesia occupies East Timor, a former Portuguese territory, despite United Nations and human rights protests, with a large military force.

1979 The Ekadasa Rudra ritual purification, which takes place once a century, is held at Besakih temple.

1986 Nusa Dua is developed into an upmarket tourist enclave.

1995 Indonesia celebrates 50 years of independence.

1997 Asian economic crisis hits Indonesia, leading to social and political unrest.

1998 Public pressures Suharto to hand over leadership to Vice President B.J. Habibi, who allows East Timor a referendum on independence.

2000 Abdurrahman Wahid is Indonesia's first democratically elected president.

2001 Vice President Megawati Sukarnoputri, daughter of the former President Sukarno, is elected President in place of the disgraced Abdurrahman Wahid. Liberals fear her close rapport with the military, which perpetrated the worst excesses of the New Order regime.

Preceding pages: on the beach at Kuta
Below: temple exhibit at the Bali Museum

1: The South

Bali's tourist 'built-up areas' are concentrated in the south. The reasons for the development of the tourist infrastructure along this previously quiet coastal strip are clear: endless beaches, the proximity of Ngurah Rai International Airport and the capital city of Denpasar. With an average density of more than 540 inhabitants per sq km (1,500 per sq mile), this area is the most heavily populated region on the island, the people drawn by the tourist boom and employment opportunities.

DENPASAR

The capital of Bali province (pop. 522,785) is also the island's economic and administrative hub. The town was previously known as Badung, and was at one stage the royal capital of the kingdom of the same name. In 1945, the administrative centre of the province of Bali was moved from Singaraja to Badung. When Indonesia declared independence, the town was rechristened Denpasar and from this point the settlement rapidly grew into a town. Most tourists avoid the traffic chaos of the capital, but it is nonetheless worth at least a short visit. The market and museum, in any case, should not be missed.

The route to the sights of Denpasar leads to the **Taman Puputan Badung** in the centre of

the town. A big field with a large bronze statue of an adult and two children, armed and going to battle, this memorial is similar to the ones found in many Balinese villages commemorating the *puputan* massacre of 1906 *(see page 22)*.

The ★ **Bali Museum** (open Tues–Thur 9am–5pm, Fri 8–11am, Sat 8am– 12.30pm and Sun 8am–2pm, closed Mon) lies to the east of the square. It provides an excellent introduction to Balinese art and culture from the early history of the island to the present day. Housed in a spacious complex created by the Dutch in 1932, the museum combines the architectural styles of palaces and temples in the north, east and west of Bali to create a colourful whole. The individual collections are divided between four buildings and contain masks, shadow puppets, ritual objects, pottery and woodcarvings as well as an attractive picture display describing the rites of passage *(see page 99)*. Of note amongst the archaeological finds and prehistoric exhibits are the stone sarcophagi. The modern building complex contains examples of traditional and modern painting and Balinese crafts.

TEMPLE AND CHURCH

From the *kulkul* (alarm drum) tower on the left of the split gate marking the museum entrance, the perspective widens to reveal the **Pura Jagatnata** to the north. In the sanctuary of this royal temple, the universal deity Sanghyang Widhi Wasa is worshipped. The deity is the symbol of faith in the one Almighty God in accordance with the Indonesian national doctrine. The massive Lotus Throne *(padmasana)* dominating the complex bears a metal relief depicting Sang Hyang Widhi Wasa dancing.

Behind the *pura* rises the tower of the Catholic **Church of St Joseph**, the entrance of which is via Jalan Kepundung. The decoration is a charming mixture of Christian pictorial details and Balinese elements. The reliefs decorating the facade are reminiscent of Balinese temples, and the angels dressed in sarongs bear a strong resemblance to Legong dancers.

Arts Festival
The Bali Arts Festival is held each year between mid-June and July. It brings artists and dancers from across the island, as well as other islands and countries, to showcase art and culture. It also encourages and develops new performing arts creations and media.

Below: Pura Jagatnata
Bottom: Church of St Joseph

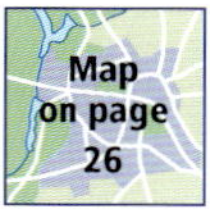

Jalan Gajah Mada and the side streets Jalan Kartini and Jalan Sulawesi bustle with life. They are full of antique and craft shops stocked with wares that are mostly cheaper than those found in the tourist centres of the island.

BUSTLING MARKETS

A stroll across to the market of ★ **Pasar Badung** allows you to immerse yourself in the everyday life of the island by observing Balinese housewives buying fresh produce. On the other side of the river lies **Pasar Kumbasari**, a sprawling centre for crafts designed to appeal to mass taste. There are a few restaurants here as well.

If you have developed a taste for Balinese art, you should visit the ★★ **Werdhi Budaya Art Centre** on Jalan Nusa Indah on the eastern edge of town (open Tues–Sun 9am– 4pm). The architecture of the individual pavilions is worth seeing in itself. Inside you will find works by Balinese painters and wood carvers, and exhibitions of items for sale are sometimes held. A separate section commemorates the work of the German artist Walter Spies.

Every evening the complex comes to life, when groups of tourists come to watch the excellent Kecak dance performances *(see page 109)*, which begin at 6.30pm.

Below: Werdhi Budaya Art Centre
Bottom: Pasar Badung market

KUTA/LEGIAN

These two fishing villages, which once lay several kilometres apart on the island's most beautiful beach on the southwest coast, were the epitome of paradise for the hippies and world travellers who arrived on Bali during the 1960s. They have long since become the largest tourist development area on the island.

No fewer than 400 dwellings, ranging from simple *losmen* (guesthouses) to international luxury hotels, shelter mostly younger tourists from the West, along with large numbers of Australians. The main tourist axis may be found along Jalan Raya Legian, the central road linking the two centres. The traffic is heavy, with an endless stream of cars and motorbikes, and along the sides, shops, restaurants, cafés, street traders, money changers and car rental companies are lined up in colourful profusion.

Star Attraction

- **Werdhi Budaya Art Centre**

Bali by the beach

If you sit long enough on Kuta Beach, all of Bali will come to you. Roving vendors offer paintings, wood carvings, sarongs, handicrafts, jewellery, massages, hair-braiding and manicures. The parade can be entertaining and annoying in turn and 'no thank you' has little affect. To avoid the swarm, move further north to Legian Beach or beyond.

A CHOICE OF BEACHES

Hordes of sun-worshippers, watersports fiends and surfers crowd **Kuta**, famous for its beach, surf and gorgeous sunsets. At night, Jalan Raya Legian comes alive with a rash of fashionable nightspots and restaurants serving everything from Italian pastas to Indonesian *nasi padang*.

Jalan Pantai Kuta, running along the beach, is quieter, and in some of the side streets linking the two roads it is still possible to find hints of Kuta's former village life. If your first instinct is to flee from the spectre of mass tourism in Kuta, and yet you want to be near it, settle for the much quieter and more relaxed **Legian**, although these days it is difficult to tell where Kuta ends and Legian begins.

Well informed travellers prefer to say at **Seminyak**, found at the northern end of Legian. The beach is just as broad and sandy here but the atmosphere is much more serene. Mostly the preserve of expensive resorts like The Legian and Oberoi, both of which are found here, as well as a clutch of good restaurants serving Italian and Mediterranean cuisines.

Surfboards at Kuta beach

SANUR

Luminaries like novelist Vicki Baum, who used **Sanur** as the setting for her book, *A Tale from Bali*, and the Belgian painter Jean Le Mayeur, put the quiet fishing village on to the world travel map during the 1930s. In 1966, the opening of the Hotel Bali Beach, built as wartime reparation by the Japanese, marked the beginning of Sanur's rapid development from a malaria-infested swamp to a world-class resort.

Below: Sanur art market
Bottom: parasailing

Relatively more sedate and expensive than Kuta, Sanur – situated on the southeast coast – has always enjoyed a more up-market image, although it is increasingly crowded with shops and restaurants. There is a selection of hotels, some with local bungalow-style accommodations, in the different price categories. As a result of the stronger tidal currents on the east coast, the water retreats as far as the offshore coral reef, making swimming almost impossible at low tide.

The ★ **Museum Le Mayeur** (open Sun–Fri 8.30am–2pm) in Sanur is the legacy left behind by the Belgian painter Jean Le Mayeur. He arrived in Bali in 1932 and is famous for his colourful Impressionist-like paintings, mainly of Ni Polok, the Balinese dancer he married. Although his paintings have suffered from the brackish sea air, the museum is worth a visit for its air of nostalgia.

NUSA DUA AND TANJUNG BENOA

Bukit (meaning 'hill') **Badung**, also known as Bukit Peninsula, at Bali's southernmost tip, is largely devoid of vegetation apart from scrub and cactus. However, standing in stark contrast is the irrigated eastern section of the peninsula, the tourist centre of **Nusa Dua**.

The enclave of Nusa Dua – which means 'two islands' – covers an area of several hundred hectares (or acres) in the east of the Bukit Badung peninsula. This self-contained area was conceived during the early 1970s, when mass tourism began to take a hold on Bali, and was partly financed with funds from the World Bank. The government's aim was to restrict tourist development to specific areas and keep the locals away from the inevitable results of mass tourism.

The project fulfilled the government's aims as far as separating tourists from the daily life of the local inhabitants is concerned. In 1983, the Nusa Dua Beach Hotel opened as the first of a series of a dozen luxury hotels in the area. It is difficult for a guest to believe that Bali is still part of the Third World when comfortably ensconced within the confines of a luxury hotel, surrounded by immaculately landscaped gardens. Pampered holidaymakers who long for sun and sand, and only the occasional taste of the island's culture, will feel at home here. Instant 'Balinese Evenings', with a buffet and dance performance, package the island's culture for visitors.

Nusa Dua continues northward into **Tanjung Benoa**, which is lined with yet more hotels, including a Club Med, as well as watersports operations.

Best catch

Jimbaran Beach turns into one, long, thriving seafood restaurant at sundown. The local catch of the day is offered from rustic beach-side restaurant stalls, often with the sea lapping only metres only. Select your fresh favourites to be grilled over aromatic coconut husks, served with rice and simple vegetables, washed down with a cold beer.

Hilton Hotel at Nusa Dua

JIMBARAN

Northwest of Bukit Badung, south of Kuta and the airport, lies the rapidly developing **Jimbaran Beach**, a relatively new resort area with a white sand crescent beach that was previously ignored by Bali's architects of tourism. Discovered only in the past decade, the beach has attracted deluxe resorts developments such as the Ritz-Carlton, Four Seasons and the Intercontinental groups. For

Map on page 26

Penida's past

According to legend, inhospitable Nusa Penida is home to demons and evil spirits. Fearless giant Jero Gede Mecaling, who brings misfortune and illness, supposedly inhabits the place. For prisoners formerly banished there by Balinese rulers, there was no worse place for exile.

Pura Uluwatu

the moment at least, one can enjoy the quiet atmosphere and the clean waters of its beach.

PURA ULUWATU

From Jimbaran, after following a winding road for about 25km (16 miles), you will reach ★★ **Pura Uluwatu**, thought to have been founded at the turn of the first millennium AD. Like Pura Tanah Lot *(see page 47)*, this is one of the six holiest temples on the island. The journey is worthwhile just to see its spectacular location on the cliffs overlooking the pounding surf.

The temple is dedicated to Dewi Danu, the ruler of the sea and the patron goddess of the lakes who, according to Balinese legend, landed on the island at Uluwatu. The rocky plateau on which the temple stands is said to be her ship, transformed into stone. A hundred metres below, huge waves dash against the rocks, but foreign surf fans are happy to ride the dangerous waves off **Suluban Beach**.

NUSA PENIDA AND NUSA LEMBONGAN

These two sparsely populated and arid islands, off Bali's southeast coast, have little in common with the tropically lush main island. **Nusa Penida** covers over 300 sq km (116sq miles) of arid limestone highlands. Fishing, maize and seaweed farming sustain the 40,000 mostly Muslim islanders. Visits to Toyapakeh or Jungutbatu fishing villages provide a glimpse of everyday life.

Smaller **Nusa Lembongan** is more inviting; its Sanggiang Bay is ringed with cozy *losmen* homestays, beach clubs and elegant boutique hotels, and is an ideal overnight escape from Bali. Spectacular snorkelling opportunities in the calm bay, or diving in the swift currents around Lembongan, Penida and smaller Ceningan islands, guarantee sightings of copious marine life.

Fishing boats make daily trips from Sanur to Nusa Penida and Nusa Lembongan, and numerous companies offer day cruises to Nusa Lembongan from Benoa Harbour.

2: Ubud and Environs

Map below

The cultural heart of Bali is a region where beautiful countryside, artistry, and life in a village community still rich in traditions, are blended into a harmonious whole. Ubud, and the surrounding villages in the central Balinese province of Gianyar, have more or less grown together as a result of rampant tourist development during the past few decades. The town itself takes its name from *ubad*, Balinese for medicine, stemming from the healing properties of herbs growing near the Campuhan River.

Star Attraction
- **Pura Uluwatu**

ARTISTIC CENTRE

Today, Ubud is the home of painters, sculptors and dancers, and this is where increasing numbers of foreign artists have made their home since the 1920s. As a result, Ubud's fame as the centre of artistic and cultural skills on the island has

Puppet paints in Ubud

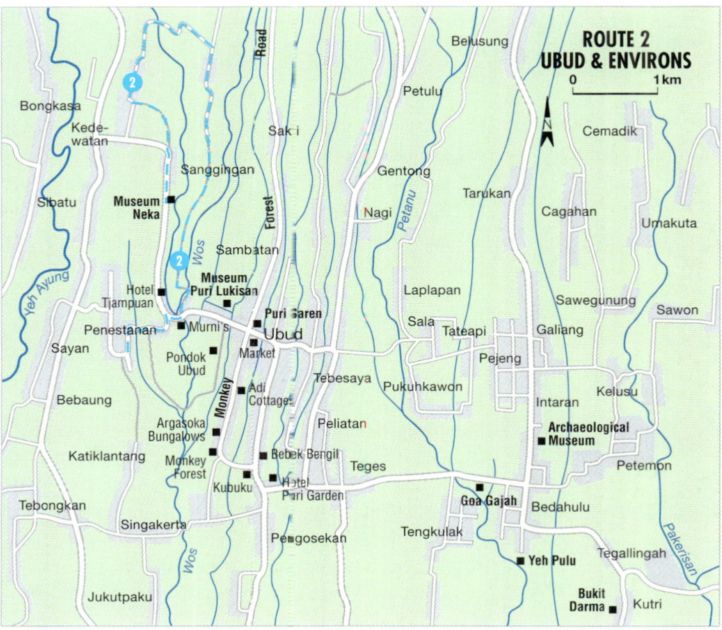

Map on page 33

> **Settling down**
> One of the most congenial, and the most inexpensive, places to stay at Ubud is at one of the *losmen* (guesthouses) run by local families. Whether you settle for this simple option of a fan-cooled room with shared facilities, or you choose one of Ubud's typical bungalow-style lodgings set in tranquil gardens ablaze with tropical flowers, you will quickly feel at home.

Ubud locals

spread rapidly throughout the West. To many visitors, Ubud is the epitome of the scenic beauty and cultural richness which characterise Bali. With a dozen temples in the area, there is a good chance to witness a few of the colourful religious temple ceremonies during your stay.

An Ideal Base

Bearing in mind the size of Ubud and its population of around 60,000, the vast range of accommodation and restaurants competing for the attention of tourists – not to mention the rampant commerce – may seem overwhelming. Visitors hoping to escape the area entirely will do well to head for the surrounding villages – like Campuhan, Sayan, Peliatan or Pengosekan – which provide a better chance of experiencing life in an authentic Balinese village community.

Having left the bustle of Jalan Ubud Raya, the main east-west artery, and **Monkey Forest Road**, which forms the main thoroughfare running from north to south, you will be in the heart of rural Bali, and can delight in the honking of geese and the breeze wafting through the rice fields.

Ubud's favourable location makes it an ideal base for excursions. You can visit some of the oldest temples on the island or explore the delights of the local countryside just by walking. The region is criss-crossed by a network of narrow but mostly well constructed roads, linking the many villages in the vicinity of Ubud with each other. With the aid of a route map, the area is also ideal for a bicycle tour.

Dances and Festivals

Visitors to Ubud can witness one of the daily dance performances, which are generally regarded as being the best the island has to offer. Information concerning the various cultural and other events, temple festivals, as well as tickets for the events themselves, can be obtained from the **Bina Wisata Tourist Centre** (tel: 361-973285) along Jalan Ubud Raya.

AYUNG RIVER RAFTING

Even sports fans will find plenty to appeal to them, as there are excellent opportunities for river rafting on the Ayung River in Sayan, near Kedewatan. The ★★ **Ayung River** is Bali's top whitewater rafting attraction. Slicing through the Sayan Valley, the river offers about 20 Class II to IV rapids for a fun day's outing with one of numerous rafting operators. It is safe and fun for rafters of all ages. Although rafting can be done throughout the year, the best thrills are during the rainy season from November to March.

Star Attraction

- **Rafting on the Ayung River**

Below: local musician
Bottom: rafting the Ayung river

FOREIGN INFLUENCES

Western painters arriving in Bali in the early 20th century sought inspiration in the tropical landscape as well as the works of the local artists. Two of the first arrivals were Walter Spies, the German painter and musician, and a Dutch artist, Rudolf Bonnet. They settled in Campuhan, in those days a separate village but today a district of Ubud, where they studied Balinese painting. During the 1930s, together with a local nobleman named Cokorde Gde Agung Sukawati, they founded an artists' association known as Pita Maha *(see page 102)*. This initiative inspired an artistic renaissance, transforming Ubud, once a sleepy village, into a centre of cultural revolution.

Map on page 33

A WEALTH OF GALLERIES

The tradition and importance of painting in Ubud can be seen not least in two of the most important art museums on the island. Would-be purchasers of art will find a useful summary of the principal genres and types of art practised in Bali. Behind the Pura Saraswati temple in the heart of the town lies the ★★ **Museum Puri Lukisan** ('Palace of Paintings'; open daily 8am–4pm). Opened in 1956, the museum owes its existence to the efforts of Rudolf Bonnet. It contains an excellent collection of Balinese painting, and traces the development of wood carving. Some of the displays here are for sale.

Visitors can either walk or take a *bemo* from the centre of Ubud to the ★★★ **Museum Neka** (open daily 9am–5pm), which lies some 2km (1 mile) north of Campuhan, on the road to Kedewatan. It is named after Suteja Neka, a native of Ubud. The son of a renowned woodcarver, Neka was an avid art collector and a member of the Pita Maha group. His museum, which opened in 1982, is aimed at educating foreigners on the development of Balinese painting, from the traditional *wayang* or *kamasan* style – commissioned as decorations in palaces and temples – to more contemporary forms of expression.

The museum's art collection is distributed between four pavilions. The first contains works

Below: gardens at the Museum Puri Lukisan
Bottom: Museum Neka, exterior detail

showing the development from the *wayang* style through the Ubud/Batuan style to representative works by the Young Artists' group *(see page 38)*.

LOCAL AND WESTERN INFLUENCES

The second pavilion is devoted to outstanding Balinese artists, including Gusti Nyoman Lempad, who died in 1978 at the age of 116. Lempad's detailed ink drawings of barong heads, cremation towers and temple reliefs influenced an entire school of art. The third pavilion displays the works of Balinese and Javanese artists who have succeeded in retaining a strong traditional accent in their work despite obvious Western influences. The last pavilion houses works by exceptional Indonesian artists, in particular those of Affandi (1907–90).

On the upper floor are works by foreign artists who were influenced by Balinese art, and who in turn influenced local painters. The collection includes paintings by the late Rudolf Bonnet and Antonio Maria Blanco, as well as Arie Smit and Han Snell, both of whom still live in Ubud. The only example of the works of Walter Spies is a copy of one of his paintings.

In the direction of Pengosekan lies the well-known ★★ **Agung Rai Museum of Art** (open daily 9am–6pm), which has an impressive collection of traditional and modern Balinese paintings, and works on Bali by foreign artists. The permanent collection should not be missed.

CAMPUHAN WALK

Visitors who want to feast their senses on Balinese landscape should embark on the three-hour ★★ **walk to Campuhan**. From Museum Neka, the path leads for about 400m (¼ mile) in a northerly direction as far as Sangingan, where it passes the Ulun Ubud Cottages before turning west. Walkers can immerse themselves in the everyday life of Bali as depicted in the paintings seen in the museum. Narrow footpaths lead between rice paddies before continuing along the main street of the village. After following the asphalt road for

Star Attractions
- Museum Puri Lukisan
- Museum Neka
- Agung Rai Museum of Art
- Walk to Campuhan

Spies seen no more
Ironically, not a single original work of Walter Spies – who together with Rudolph Bonnet was responsible for introducing Western art aesthetics and methods to the Balinese in the 1920s – has remained on the island. All of Spies pictures, each one worth a small fortune, are today found in private collections elsewhere in the world.

Museum Neka exhibit

Map on page 33

a short way, the path turns around a long bend and crosses a bridge before coming to the most attractive section of all, above the River Uos.

After about 3km (2 miles), the route joins the main road from Ubud to Campuhan, not far from the bridge which crosses the Uos. Conveniently located beside the bridge is Murni's Warung, where you can stop for refreshments, or else head for the restaurant at the nearby Hotel Campuhan. Walter Spies lived here at the end of the 1930s, until the stream of visitors became too much for him and he retired to Iseh in the Karangasem area.

The walk can be continued from Campuhan. From the bridge there is a narrow path leading uphill away from the main road. The track leads between the rice paddies to **Penestanan**, which is reached after about 30 minutes. During the 1960s, the village was a gathering place for local schoolchildren and young people who admired the work of Dutch painter Arie Smit. The group came to be known as the 'Young Artists', and produced its own characteristic style of painting.

Shopping paradise
Ubud is a great shopping stop. The village roadways are lined with increasingly upscale shops selling home interiors and antiques, paintings and sculptures, curios and souvenirs, garments and jewellery – virtually everything the island has to offer in an open-air shopping 'mall' along the streets.

Working the paddies near Penestanan

Other Ubud Attractions

Back in the centre of Ubud, the ★ **market** provides an excellent opportunity to marvel at the array of tropical fruit. Souvenir hunters will find the market particularly good for inexpensive trinkets and crafts. Be sure to get there early though as it slows down by 2pm.

To the north of the market lies **Puri Saren**, the residence of the princely Sukawati family. The palace, with its gateways and courtyards, is still partly inhabited today, although one wing has been turned into a hotel.

Monkey Forest Road leads away from the centre in a southerly direction. About 2km (1 mile) long, it is bordered on both sides by restaurants, shops and hotels. At the beginning of the 1980s it was just a quiet village street, but now it demonstrates all too clearly the extent to which development has taken a toll on the environment. It's best to do this walk in the early morning or late afternoon because the midday sun is merciless.

At ★ **Monkey Forest** (open daily during daylight hours) visitors come face to face with a band of half-tame grey monkeys. Vendors sell bananas and packets of peanuts just outside the forest entrance, but the temptation to feed the animals should be resisted because they tend to be aggressive and have been known to bite people. Take pains to conceal any items that can be easily snatched by the monkeys – like spectacles, earrings and handbags. The local inhabitants revere the monkeys, whom they regard as the sacred descendants of the monkey general Hanuman.

A FOREST TEMPLE

Descending the steps from the entrance into the forest, it is hard not to be enchanted by the vast waringin tree, regarded as sacred by the Balinese. To the right of the tree is the temple of the underworld, the ★ **Pura Dalem Agung Padangtegal**. Its covered gateway, leading to the inner temple courtyard, stands on the back of the giant tortoise Bedawang. Entwined by two snakes, the gateway symbolises the underworld. Temples of death are dedicated to Durga, the goddess of death, who also assumes the form of the witch Rangda. Indicative of this fact are the stone Rangda sculptures, whose huge hanging breasts touch the ground and are said to guarantee fertility.

Below: encounter at Monkey Forest
Bottom: Pura Dalem Agung Padangtegal

Bali Sea
Kubutambahan
Sangsit
Air Sanih
Singaraja
Pura Jagaraga
Sawan
Lovina Beach
Gitgit
S.Daya
Sambirenteng
Kalibukbuk
Seririt
Tangguwesia
Banjar
Pengastulan
Brahma Vihara
Mayong
Busungbiyu
Danau Buyan
Danau Tamblingan
Danau Bratan
Munduk
Candi Kuning
Pura Ulun Danu
Bedugul
Pura Tegeh Koripan
Penulisan
Sangan
Gunung Batur 1717
Toya Bungkah
Kintamani
Batur
Danau Batur
Terunyan
Penelokan
Gunung Abang 2153
Pelaga
Pupuan
Gunung Batukau 2276
Baturiti
Pura Luhur
Pempatan
Batukau
Petanu
Pura Besakih
Blimbing
Penebel
Kukup
Sebatu
Tirtha Empul
Payangan
Tampaksiring
Rendang
Tegalalang
Pura Gunung Kawi
Tembuku
Bangli
Yehunda
Tunjuk
Marga
Kidewatan
Petulu
Pakerisan
Sangeh
Wanasari
Alas Kedaton
Yeh He
Antosari
Miling
Ubud
Pejeng
Yeh Ayung
Semarapura (Klungkung)
Blayu
Puri Krambitan
Peliatan
Goa Gajah
Yeh Pulu
Pura Dalem Sidan
Krambitan
Tabanan
Mengwi
Mas
Kutri
Gianyar
Kusamba
Gelgel
Bona
Kapal
Lukluk
Celuk
Sukawati
Sempidi
Tanah Lot
Batubulan
Badung
Denpasar
INDIAN OCEAN
Braban
Sanur
Jungutbatu
Nusa Lembongan
Semawang
Selat
Legian
Nusa Ceningan
Kuta
Pulau Serangan
Benoa Port
Jimbaran
Nusa Dua
Uluwatu
Bukit Badung

Navigating Bali
Bali's size and the apparent proximity of locations can be deceiving. Narrow roadways, traffic congested by tour buses and ceremonial processions, other road obstacles such as potholes, and the pace of life can affect travel plans. Allow twice the time you think is necessary to reach a destination and make the journey leisurely, avoiding tight schedules and frustration. Life goes at its own pace in Bali.

Below: Brahma Vihara Monastery (see page 76)
Bottom: Pura Taman Ayun detail (see page 43)

Map on pages 40–41

3: Temples of Mountain and Sea

Mengwi – Alas Kedaton – Marga – Gunung Batukau – Pura Luhur – Tanah Lot

The journey to the holy places of mountain and sea leads from the sea *(kelod)*, the realm of the demons, towards the mountains of the island's interior *(kaja)*, the home of the gods. On the way you will pass three very different temples. The Taman Ayun in Mengwi is one of the loveliest on Bali, while Pura Luhur's mysterious location at the foot of the volcano Gunung Batukau makes it a worthwhile attraction. At the final temple, Tanah Lot, both the dramatic setting of jagged-edged cliffs and crashing waves, and the temple silhouetted against the setting sun, will enthrall. This full-day excursion leads through a landscape of mountains alternating with rice terraces – set out early and return before nightfall.

Below: rice paddies
Bottom: artist at Pura Taman Ayun

VILLAGE ATTRACTIONS

Visitors approaching from Nusa Dua or Kuta will skirt Denpasar, the island's bustling capital, on its northwestern fringes. Those coming from Sanur should follow the ring road to the north and east of the town before setting out in the direction of Mengwi and Tanah Lot. Eventually, the metropolis is left behind and new perspectives open up.

In the more densely populated parts of the island, some stretches of road lead through an endless succession of villages which seem to form a single built-up area. In the villages bordering the route are countless examples of the artistic creativity of the Balinese. In ★**Kapal**, for instance, the road runs through what appears to be a sculpture garden surrounded by the workshops of potters and stonemasons. For generations, the village craftsmen here have created the elaborate decorative fixtures which adorn Balinese temples and house fronts throughout the island.

★

Star Attraction

● Pura Taman Ayun

Ceramic centre
Pejaten village, south of Tabanan town, is a centre of ceramic works. Many cottage industry operations produce decorative dishes, ornaments and pots, while others concentrate on roof tiles and home or temple ornamentation from red clay.

PURA TAMAN AYUN

A few kilometres further on (17km/11 miles from Denpasar), a turning on the right leads to ★★★ **Pura Taman Ayun**. This is the second most important temple in Bali (after Pura Besakih, *see page 61*). Visitors wishing to experience its peaceful ceremonial atmosphere should aim to arrive as early as possible, before the hordes of tourists descend. In the early hours of the morning, it will seem as if nothing could interrupt the tranquillity of the custodian who bends over his short-handled broom, sweeping up the leaves and blossoms from the frangipani tree.

Below: Pura Taman Ayun

HARMONIOUS ARCHITECTURE

As you enter the first courtyard, your gaze will be drawn towards the *kulkul* bell tower to the left of the main gateway. A narrow staircase leads up to a broad platform which provides the best view of the complex. With its clearly defined division into three terraced courtyards, the Pura Taman Ayun is a perfect example of the harmonious principles underlying Balinese temple architecture. Surrounded by moats covered with lotus blossoms, the 'Garden Temple on the Water' stands on an artificial island. The term *taman* is reserved for temples which are at least partly surrounded by water.

The Pura Taman Ayun is dedicated to the Widadari, the 'heavenly nymphs' sent from

Map on pages 40–41

Royal temple
The Pura Taman Ayun is one of the so-called 'royal temples', and as such is held in awe by all Balinese. Its importance goes back to I Gusti Agung Anom, a member of a minor branch of the Gelgel dynasty who founded the once-powerful kingdom of Mengwi in the 18th century.

heaven to bathe at this spot. In the southwestern corner of the complex is a square basin surrounded by demons. They mark the points of the compass and indicate the boundaries of the underworld. To the north, a series of terraces ascends the mountainside towards the home of the gods.

The *jeroan* is the highest and most sacred courtyard. It is not open to visitors, but contains 29 shrines, some of them elaborately decorated with up to 11 meru roofs *(see page 97)*. These symbolise the trees of heaven as they soar skywards into the realm of the gods, inviting them to descend to earth. Here, too, stands the triple lotus throne, the *padmasana*, which is the seat of honour reserved for the *trimurti*, the trinity of the three principal deities Shiva, Vishnu and Brahma. Several smaller, more modest shrines are dedicated to various mountain deities.

Gifts at the Alas Kedaton Monkey Forest

ANOTHER MONKEY FOREST

Leave the temple and return through Mengwi to the junction at which you originally turned off. Turning right here, the route continues along the main road towards Bedugul (Lake Bratan) and Singaraja. After about 3km (2 miles), turn left in a westerly direction (look out for the sign to Marga) along a minor road which leads towards Peken and arrives shortly at the **Alas Kedaton Monkey Forest**.

The Balinese believe that the hundreds of grey monkeys living in the trees here are the descendants of the brave troops of the legendary monkey general, Hanuman. Unlike the monkeys in the forest of Sangeh, who are often disturbed by visitors and are therefore much more aggressive, the monkeys of Alas Kedaton are less daunting. A walk through the forest provides good opportunities to observe their habits.

MARGA MAGIC

Turning your back on the monkeys in the woods and the traders in the forest of stalls around the entrance, continue to ★ **Marga**. Here, Balinese history comes alive on the drive along the wide approach road to the memorial. Surrounded by a broad lawn, the monument to the island's heroes radiates an aura of melancholy peace.

The inscriptions recall the events of 20 November 1946, which turned Marga into the setting for a *puputan* *(see page 23)*, in this instance the ritual suicide of a band of Balinese resistance fighters under their general I Gusti Ngurah Rai. A Buddhist reliquary was erected to honour the fallen soldiers on the adjoining cemetery. The exhibits and photographs in the little museum tell the moving tale of the Balinese and Indonesian independence struggle more graphically than anywhere else on the island.

Below and bottom: Marga, monument to the island's heroes

MOUNTAINS AND RICE TERRACES

From Marga, the narrow road, poorly maintained in places, continues westwards as far as Tunjuk. Here, it turns towards the south and, after passing through Beng and Calagi, eventually joins the better surfaced main road north to **Gunung Batukau**. Take care not to miss the turning at Sekartaji. Continuing up towards the summit of the second-highest mountain on Bali (2,276m/7,467ft), the road leads the way to the home of the gods across the peaks of the central mountain chain.

By the early afternoon, the mountain peaks often retreat from view behind a thick curtain of clouds. The rice-terrace landscape, formed by human hands from the fertile volcanic soil, resembles a vast sculpture. Supported by clay walls, the narrow terraces of rice paddies curve gently as they follow the contours of the hillside. In some places they rise up the slopes gradually, whilst in others they climb steeply toward the summit.

Where the fields are flooded but not yet planted, the clouds and palm fronds will be reflected in the water's surface. In other fields, the young rice seedlings gleam emerald green in the sunlight as far as the eye can see. For many visitors, it's a perfect photo opportunity.

Below and bottom: Pura Luhur Batukau and deity

PURA LUHUR BATUKAU

The journey continues uphill along a gently curving road for another 20km (13 miles) as far as ★**Pura Luhur Batukau**, the 'Coconut Shell Mountain'. The temple lies on the southeastern flank of the volcano. The last section of road from Wongaya Gede to the temple itself, situated some 3km (2 miles) above the village, was widened in 1993 to improve access to the mountain temple, which was restored during the same year. The spacious complex extends across several levels on the hillside. It is an awe-inspiring location in a clearing surrounded by jungle. In the mossy stupa-like shrines you cannot help but sense the presence of Maha Dewi, the 'Spirit of the Mountain', who is worshipped here on festival days.

An artificial pond on the right-hand side of the complex is reminiscent of Pura Taman Ayun in Mengwi *(see page 43)*. Like Taman Ayun, Pura Luhur is a 'national' temple. On special feast days, such as Galungan, which celebrates the victory of good over evil, crowds of brightly clothed pilgrims gather here to pray.

TABANAN

Visitors should start their return journey no later than 4pm. The first stage of the route heads south, reaching **Tabanan**, the capital of the administrative district of the same name, after 27km (17 miles). Continue for a short distance along the main road towards Denpasar to arrive at the Tanah Lot turning, which lies just north of Kediri. Tabanan is the rice bowl of Bali, and, in this typically rice-farming countryside, travellers will be able to glimpse the lifestyle of its inhabitants.

Star Attraction
- Pura Tanah Lot

TANAH LOT SUNRISE

When the light is right, a Balinese sunset is a dramatic natural phenomenon. Legend has it that the ★★★ **Pura Tanah Lot**, perched on a rocky outcrop above the sea, was founded by Hindu priest Danghyang Nirartha in the 16th century.

Pura Tanah Lot is one of the island's six most holy temples, and one of a series of protective shrines along the south coast dedicated to deities of the sea.

Balinese from across the island bring offerings here to placate the demons inhabiting the sea. One of the most photographed icons of the island, it is a perfect sunset stop, albeit marred by the presence of numerous cafes and drinks stalls. During high tide, the rocky outcrop on which the temple sits becomes flooded with sea water – thankfully, a plan to build a footbridge to the temple years ago was rejected.

Guardian snakes
The caves and rocks surrounding Pura Tanah Lot swarm with poisonous snakes. Locals say that the snakes – transformed magically by the temple's founder, Hindu priest Danghyang Nirartha from his waist sash – guard the temple against evil intruders. Be careful if you decide to cross over.

Tanah Lot sunrise

Map on pages 40–41

4: The Craftsmen's Road

Batubulan – Celuk – Mas – Peliatan – Ubud

A stroll through the workshops and galleries fringing the road from Batubulan to Peliatan will emphasise the importance of art in the everyday life of the Balinese, whether you attend a *Barong* performance or a stonemason's studio in Batubulan, a silversmith's workshop in Celuk or admire the skills of the woodcarvers of Mas. For a change of scenery from the south, move up to Ubud *(see page 33)*, which together with the surrounding villages is still the centre of Balinese painting. There is about one hour of driving on this route.

Below: Pura Puseh Batubulan
Bottom: Barong dance at Batubulan

A STONEMASONS' VILLAGE

Batubulan lies only a few kilometres from the tourist centres of the south coast. Countless stone sculptures lined up along the roadside leave the visitor in no doubt that this is the centre of Balinese stonemasonry. Hindu gods and heroes stand here beside Buddha heads, gnomes and other mythical creatures. The larger examples of these elaborately carved sandstone or Andesite lavastone figures can be seen in hotels and restaurants throughout the island. However, the galleries and workshops also contain many works of art small enough to fit into a suitcase.

Temple decoration was the stonemason's preserve, but today frequent recourse is made to more permanent and cheaper cement castings. It is no coincidence, however, that Batubulan is the home of a temple, the ★ **Pura Puseh Batubulan**, which is adorned with one of the finest examples of the stonemasons' art. The two Buddha statues in niches on either side of the entrance are no doubt derived from the temple of Borobudur on Java. In any case, they indicate that the founder of the Buddhist teaching is entitled to a place in the Balinese pantheon of gods.

Bird and Reptile Parks

Just past the junction beyond Batubulan, the north fork leads to Singapadu, where the ★★ **Bali Bird Park** (open daily 9am–6pm) is the island's best animal attraction. Two hectares (5 acres) of botanical gardens are filled with more than 1,000 tropical birds – some 250 species – from throughout Indonesia and the world. With many endangered and rare species, this is one of the few places to see Bali starlings and birds of paradise. A walk-through aviary simulates a rainforest, with birds flying free for close inspection.

Next door, **Rimba Reptile Park** houses many of the world's most deadly creatures, with over 160 animals, including an 8-metre (26-ft) reticulated python, said to be the largest in captivity.

Barong and Rangda

Batubulan's other main attraction is the ★★★ **Barong Dance** *(see page 109)*. The stage is the oldest of four in the village. For more than 20 years, Barong and Rangda have fought here every morning between 9.30 and 10.30am. The exorcist ritual has become a tourist show, but it is so accurately executed that it is a must for every visitor. Those wishing to see the temple in peace, however, should arrive before 9am or after 11am.

The antique shops along the main road look tempting, but many of the so-called genuine items for sale are no more than a few months old.

Star Attractions
- **Bali Bird Park**
- **Barong Dance**

Darling starling
One of Bali's few endemic creatures, the striking *Leucopsar Rothschildi*, or the Bali starling, is on the brink of vanishing, with less than 15 remaining in the wild. Captive breeding programmes hope to regenerate Bali starlings on the island and educate the population to protect this endangered bird.

Below: Barong band
Bottom: a dancer's mask

Map on pages 40–41

Jewellery fans should not miss ⋆ **Celuk**, only 2 km (3 miles) further north. The village is home to the island's gold- and silversmiths. The biggest galleries are on the main street, but bargain hunting is more fun in the little family-run businesses in the side streets, where you can watch craftsmen producing their delicate wares.

Sukawati stop

The Sukawati art market past Celuk along the main road, is famous for fine basket work and colourful wood carvings, especially realistic tropical fruits from soft wood. The morning market, behind the art market and to the east, wholesales in bulk every handicraft imaginable. Open only until 10am.

SUKAWATI AND MAS

Sukawati is home to the most famous puppeteers *(dalang)* on Bali. Their remarkable skills *(see page 106)* have not yet been exploited commercially. The village also boasts a colourful fruit and vegetable market. Near Sakah, leave the main road where it bends to the east. Continue straight ahead for a few kilometres to arrive in ⋆ **Mas**. More Brahman families live here than anywhere else on the island. They can trace their origins back to the Javanese priest Nirartha, who established the caste system on Bali in the 16th century.

Nowadays, Mas is better known as the village of woodcarvers. Unfortunately, commerce has won the battle against art for its own sake, and the range of galleries is bewildering. The exhibits are expensive and adapted to suit Western tastes. Nonetheless, the craftsmanship is excellent, and the local artisans guarantee that they use ebony, in contrast to the cheap imitations in the markets, which are made of sawo wood dyed with shoe polish. The latter is likely to develop cracks as soon as it is transported to temperate climes.

Below: silver shop sign in Celuk
Bottom: woodcarver in Mas

PELIATAN

Peliatan is already a suburb of Ubud, whose proximity can be deduced from the numerous art galleries and craftsmen's shops. Peliatan, however, is more famous as the home of dance groups which always win the first prize in the annual Legong dance competition *(see page 109)*. The Bina Wisata Tourist Office in Ubud *(see page 118)* has information and organises coach trips to Peliatan's two dance theatres.

Further on, a west turn leads back to Ubud.

5: Bali's Oldest Shrines

Ubud – Tegalalang – Tampaksiring – Gunung Kawi – Pejeng – Yeh Pulu – Goa Gajah

Map on pages 40–41

Travel through the spectacular Tegalalang valley, with its startling views of lush rice terraces, before visiting some of Bali's oldest temples and the world's largest kettle drum at Pejeng. Lovers of antiquities will enjoy the archaeological museum at Bedulu, the mysterious rock reliefs of Yeh Pulu and the meditation cave of Goa Gajah. This tour will easily take several hours, and therefore requires an early morning start.

Star Attraction
- Rice terraces near Tegalalang

Below: white heron at Petulu
Bottom: goose herdsman at Tegalalang

HERONS AND RICE TERRACES

Leave Ubud in a northerly direction on the minor road to **Petulu**. At this hour the little village has no special attractions to offer but plan to return one day at about 5pm, when hundreds of *kokokan* (white herons) return to roost in the trees after spending the day searching for food in the surrounding rice fields. Watch from a safe distance if you do not fancy being rained upon by messy bird droppings.

The next stage of the journey is very picturesque. After a few kilometres, near the village of **Tegalalang**, the route passes through artistically designed ★★ **rice terraces** clinging

Map on pages 40–41

to the slopes above a river valley. It is obvious that travelling vendors have already worked out that this is a popular place with tourists: they lie in wait for visitors who stop to survey the scene. Most of the items on sale will be the brightly coloured wood carvings, for which the village of Tegalalang is famous.

TWIN WATER TEMPLES

Below: jackfruit tree at Pura Tirtha Empul
Bottom: temple guardian

Further north near Sebatu is **Pura Tirtha Gunung Kawi**, a temple dedicated to the goddess of Lake Batur. The moss-covered walls and statues look much older than they really are. Ritual bathing takes place at an adjacent pool, with water flowing in from spouts placed around it. The complex affords a pleasant respite off the beaten tourist track.

A few kilometres to the east, near Tampaksiring, lies a more famous spring sanctuary, the ★ **Pura Tirtha Empul**, which lies on the upper reaches of the Pakerisan River. The spring in the centre of the temple is said to have been struck by the god Indra himself, thereby granting the heavenly hordes immortality.

Even today, the waters which feed the ritual bathing area at the front of the complex are said to possess remarkable powers. For many centuries, on a particular day of the year, a stone found in one of the nearby villages bearing old Balinese inscriptions was ritually washed, together with masks and other cult objects, in order to renew their magic powers.

Only a few years ago, however, did scholars manage to decipher the text, which makes reference to the foundation of the temple which was built in the year 962AD. The central pools have not been used as public bathing places since the end of the 1960s. The best view of the bathing section and the adjoining temple was once the prerogative of President Sukarno, who ruled from 1945 to 1968 and had a summer palace built above the complex. Rumour has it that Sukarno used to spy on naked bathing beauties from his superior point.

PURA GUNUNG KAWI

Return to the main road in the direction of Pejeng, retracing the route in a southerly direction. Along the way are some very interesting archaeological sites, which bear witness to the wealth of the first recorded Balinese dynasty, which had its capital in Pejeng in the 10th and 11th centuries.

★★ **Pura Gunung Kawi** can provide another highlight of the trip, both scenically and artistically. However, you first have to descend the 300 steep steps to enjoy the view, which opens up to reveal a lovely green valley flanked by precipitous rock walls. The effort of the descent is also rewarded by nine huge rock *candi (see below)*. Four lie on one side of the river, to the left at the base of the steps, while the other five are on the opposite bank and can be reached by a bridge.

These *candi* are often described as royal tombs, although no traces of human remains have ever been found to support the view that this is a burial ground.

MONUMENTS TO KINGS

The term *candi* is Javanese, and was derived from a name of the Hindu goddess Durga, who was associated with a cult of the dead. Unlike in Bali, where the ashes of the deceased are scattered in the sea, Javanese *candi* are mostly mausoleums

Star Attraction
- Pura Gunung Kawi

Giant efforts
Pura Gunung Kawi is said to be the work of the giant Kebo Iwo, who scratched it out with his fingernails during a single night. He also reputedly carved the reliefs at Yeh Pulu in Gianyar *(see page 56)*.

Below: rice offerings
Bottom: Pura Gunung Kawi

Map on pages 40–41

Below: Gunung Kawi view
Bottom: candi close-up

to hold the dead. In contrast to the Javanese variety, however, the *candi* of Gunung Kawi, which are nothing more than carved reliefs and which have no inner space, may have served simply as monuments in honour of Balinese kings. They have massive stepped roofs and stand some 7m (23ft) high in rock niches.

Inscriptions, in a script which was used only between the late 10th and 11th centuries, have enabled the monuments to be dated with accuracy. Deciphering the text, however, is difficult, not just because of the cryptic language, but also because the stones are badly weathered.

Scholars still can't agree on which king is commemorated here. Some claim that the monuments were erected in honour of King Udayana and his family, especially his consort, Queen Mahendradatta. The latter was a princess from east Java who was largely responsible for bringing Javanese customs to the Balinese royal court in the 11th century. It was also due to Mahendradatta's influence that Old Javanese was adopted as the language of the court. The magic rites, which play an important part in Balinese religion and were derived from Indian Tantrism, were probably brought to the island by the Javanese.

JAVANESE INFLUENCE

Other experts regard the nine *candi* as a monument for Anak Wungsu, the brother of the famous Airlangga, and his eight wives or concubines. What is clear, though, is that the monument remains one of the most tangible examples of Javanese influence on Bali's culture. From the modest-looking temple beside the group of five *candi*, visitors can enter a labyrinth-like sanctuary, which probably was once a monastery. Together with a number of hermits' cells hewn into the rock, it hints at the important role which monks must have played in those days.

Having ascended the steps once more, visitors can stop off at the nearby Restaurant Tampaksiring for a midday break before returning to the main road.

THE MOON OF PEJENG

Pejeng is the next stop along the route. More than 40 temples containing well-preserved archaeological remains bear witness to the fact that it was here that Warmadeva, the first recorded Balinese king, founded a dynasty from which King Udayana was also descended.

One attraction here is the ★ **Moon of Pejeng** in the **Pura Penataran Sasih**, thought to be the largest existing prehistoric bronze kettle drum in the world. It hangs high up in a shrine in the northwest corner of the temple. Cast in a single piece, it is both feared and revered by the Balinese.

Bali moon

The Moon of Pejeng is believed to be one of 13 legendary moons in the universe, which fell from heaven into the branches of a tree in Bali, turning night into day. According to lore, a thief climbed the tree to extinguish the moon by urinating on it. The moon exploded and fell to the ground, instantly killing the villain.

ORIGINS OF THE DRUM

There are a number of theories concerning its origin. The most plausible traces the kettle drum back to the Dongsong culture, one of Indonesia's earliest civilisations, which spread across the whole of southeast Asia from Vietnam.

No one quite knows why this ancient kettle drum was placed so high up. Anyone who wants to inspect it closely will need a telescope to make out the exquisite decorations on its stylised surface. Whatever the truths concerning its origins, it is certain that this masterpiece was made in Indonesia and dates from the 3rd century BC.

Many of the other temple shrines in Pejeng

Below: shrine housing the Moon of Pejeng
Bottom: Pura Penataran Sasih

Map on pages 40–41

are decorated with stone objects hundreds of years old, including figures of deities and representations of *linga-yoni* forms, where the *linga* represents the male and the *yoni* the female principle.

Burying their dead
The prehistoric coffins on display at Bedulu's Museum Purbakala Gedong Arca indicate that the ancient Balinese used to bury their dead – long before the Buddhists and Hindus introduced cremation.

AN ARCHAEOLOGICAL MUSEUM

The ★ **Museum Purbakala Gedong Arca** (open Tues–Sun 8.30am–2pm) is a small museum dedicated to archaeology in **Bedulu**, to the south of Pejeng on the way to the reliefs of Yeh Pulu. It contains a number of fine sarcophagi, some in the shape of animals, which date from the 2nd and 3rd centuries BC.

The name of the village is of interest too, as it is derived from Bedahulu, which means 'exchanged head', and recalls the story of Raja Ratna Banten of the Pejeng dynasty. This ruler was reputed to possess magic powers, and to prove it, he periodically allowed someone to decapitate him. On one occasion his powers failed him and his despairing servant placed a pig's head on his shoulders.From then on, no one was permitted to see the head of the Raja. However, the prime minister of the Majapahit Kingdom of Java, Gajah Mada, caught a glimpse of the deformed king, who was then literally consumed by flaming rage because of this act of impudence.

Below: Balinese smiles
Bottom: priestess at Yeh Pulu

RELIEFS OF YEH PULU

Outside Bedulu village is an interesting 10-minute walk across the rice fields to the mysterious reliefs of ★★ **Yeh Pulu**. In 1925, a relief frieze was excavated here, 27m (88ft) long and 2m (6½ft) high. Dating the find has proven extraordinarily difficult as nothing comparable has ever been found on either Bali or Java. Most experts consider the Yeh Pulu reliefs to date from the 14th century, just before the Javanese invasion.

The reliefs show scenes from daily life: a man carrying palm wine, bejewelled women, playful animals and a bear hunt. The latter gave rise to speculation that the carvings may depict scenes from the *Krishnayana*, the story of Krishna, an incarnation of the Hindu god Vishnu. The only god which can be clearly made out is the elephant-headed Ganesha, the god of wisdom. Although Ganesha no longer plays an important role in Balinese religious life, he is nonetheless presented every day with offerings by the temple priestess.

Star Attractions
● Yeh Pulu
● Goa Gajah

GOA GAJAH CAVE

★★ **Goa Gajah**, the 'Elephant Cave', is found further along the main road. The stone monster adorning the entrance to the cave, excavated in the 1920s, is hardly likely to arouse much fear – despite its bulging, squinting eyes and unkempt mane – as it prances amidst an army of animals and gnomes. Exactly who or what has been immortalised here in stone remains a mystery.

By walking through the monster's mouth, visitors enter the throat of a T-shaped cave which may once have been a hermitage for Shivaist monks. The cave is airless and dark (bring a torch). It contains a triple *linga* symbolising Shiva. There is also a Ganesha image which probably gave the cave its name, for there have never been elephants on Bali. The open-air bathing quarters in front of the cave, with its heavenly nymphs spouting water, were discovered in the 1950s.

From Goa Gajah it is a few minutes' drive back to Ubud, and an hour to Sanur or Kuta.

Below: nymphs at Goa Gajah
Bottom: reliefs at Yeh Pulu

Map on pages 40–41

6: To the East

Gianyar – Klungkung – Pura Besakih – Rendang – Putung – Candidasa

Below: rice paddies of Eastern Bali
Bottom: Ikat lengths at Gianyar

This journey to the former royal capital and to the 'Mother Temple' leads to terrifying paintings in the courtrooms of Klungkung and the most sacred temples on the island. Apart from these highlights, east Bali also provides beautiful landscapes. You can go for walks across broad terraced rice fields, and the northeast coast lures visitors with unspoilt sandy beaches. The journey from Pura Besakih, the temple of heaven, to Amlapura crosses some of the loveliest scenery on the island. At Taman Tirthagangga (*tirtha* means 'holy water', *gangga*, the Ganges), travellers can swim in the spring-fed pool of this magnificent former water palace.

DIFFERENT OPTIONS

Visitors wishing to return to South Bali on the same day should take the route via Candidasa, and continue along the southeast coast, stopping at the bat cave of Goa Lawah, and Kusamba *(see pages 66–7)*. Those with enough time to spend a few days in the east should try and stay by the beach in Candidasa. Using Candidasa as a base, you can make excursions to Amlapura, the main town of the Karangasem regency, the water palaces of

Taman Ujung and Taman Tirthagangga, and to the ancient Balinese village of Tenganan.

If starting in Ubud or the south, drive eastwards through **Bona**, where there are numerous rattan furniture factories, and then through the textile centre of **Gianyar**. After about 25km (16 miles), you will arrive in **Klungkung** (formerly Semarapura), which recently reverted to its original name.

Kamasan paintings
The village of Kamasan lies a short distance from Klungkung. Artists here, using bamboo brushes and natural pigments, are inspired by themes from Javanese mythology. The two-dimensional figures resemble *wayang* puppets from Javanese shadow drama.

KLUNGKUNG

Klungkung is a bustling provincial capital which has played an important role in the history of Bali. When the refugees belonging to the Javanese Majapahit dynasty arrived on the island during the 11th century, they made their new home in the little village of Gelgel, 3km (2 miles) south of present-day Klungkung. The son of the Majapahit ruler declared himself King of Bali and founded the Gelgel dynasty. During the 6th century, when Gelgel lost its supremacy as ruler of the island, Bali disintegrated into a series of independent principalities, many of which spent most of their time at war with the others.

In 1710, the seat of government was moved to Klungkung. The Raja of Gelgel remained the highest-ranking amongst the island princes, and his new palace became the cultural centre of the island. The prince had his own personal troupe of dancers and musicians, and gold- and silversmiths, as well as weapon forgers skilled in the art of making the traditional *keris*. His artists, centred in nearby Kamasan, founded the *wayang* or *kamasan* style of painting *(see page 102)*.

Below and bottom: stages of rattan production in Bona

TWIN PAVILIONS

However, the rule of the rajas of Klungkung came to an end when the Dutch arrived on a punitive expedition as they had done two years ago in Badung. The Raja, his family and many faithful followers committed *puputan* or ritual suicide, and the royal palace, **Puri Semarapura**, was almost completely destroyed by the vengeful Dutch. Following the destruction, two *bale*

Map on pages 40–41

Below: Puri Semapura
Bottom: the Bale Kambang

(pavilions) were expertly restored. Not only do they give insight into traditional Balinese Kamasan-painting style, they are an indication of the palace's former grandeur.

★★ **Bale Kerta Gosa**, the Hall of Justice, stands in the eastern corner, on Jalan Untung Surapati. It once housed the island's supreme court. The customary law of the land *(adat)*, which was handed down by word of mouth, varied from island to island and sometimes even from village to village. To this day, Indonesia remains a country with relatively few written laws. Conflicts are normally dealt with in the first instance by the village community, and the opposing parties only go to court if agreement cannot be reached.

Bali's Supreme Court, presided over by three Brahmans, was situated in Klungkung until the arrival of the Dutch. The punishments meted out to the guilty were draconian, as can be seen from the Kamasan-style paintings on the ceiling, which recall Christian portrayals of the Apocalypse, depicting women passing through fire as they gaze upon the faces of their aborted foetuses, adulterers whose genitals are burned away, or thieves suffering an unspeakable end in cauldrons of boiling oil. The uppermost rows, by contrast, portray the joys of heaven. This pictorial representation of the Balinese view of the world shows heaven and hell as two essential components of the universe.

The adjoining **Bale Kambang** or Floating Pavilion, located in the middle of the lotus pond, has ceilings which are also decorated with paintings. These depict the story of Prince Sutasoma defeating a man-eating demon. The building probably served as a reception or assembly hall.

Another Puputan Monument

To continue the journey to Pura Besakih, leave Klungkung in a northerly direction, passing the **Monument Puputan Klungkung**, which commemorates the ritual suicide, or *puputan*, of the Klungkung royal family.

The road climbs gently at first, and with luck the sky may be cloudless so that you have a clear view of Gunung Agung. Framed by rice fields, the silhouette of the sacred volcano appears powerful and mysterious. Here and there the paddy fields are interspersed with fields of maize, soy beans, peanuts or chillies.

When you reach the **Bukit Jambal** observation point, the road is bordered by clove trees and coffee plantations. The gradient soon becomes steeper and the bends sharper, and Gunung Agung may occasionally disappear into the clouds. The evidence of the volcano's last eruption is still clearly visible in the streams of lava which have left their black traces along the river beds.

Star Attractions
- Bale Kerta Gosa
- Pura Besakih

Snakeskin *salak*
From the vendors around Pura Besakih or along the roadway, stop and buy *salak*, also known as snakeskin fruit, grown in this region. A favourite with Indonesians, the crisp, cream-coloured fruit surrounding a large stone tastes like a cross between an apple and a pear.

PURA BESAKIH

There is a large car park outside the temple complex. Early in the morning it appears abandoned, but by noon it will be filled with coaches and lorries. The last kilometre of the journey must be completed on foot, and the countless souvenir shops lining the route make it difficult to assume the correct devotional posture. By the time pilgrims reach the main temple complex of ★★★ **Pura Besakih**, many will be out of breath and perspiring. In fact, the 'Mother Temple' is not a single edifice but rather a vast area containing more than 30 temple complexes which house more than 200 different buildings.

Below: snakeskin fruit
Bottom: Pura Besakih

Map on pages 40–41

The individual shrines still bear, in some cases, their Old Balinese names, and not even the Hindu priests are in agreement as to their true significance. Pura Besakih is to the Balinese Hindu what St Peter's in Rome is to the Roman Catholic. Its location is unique, for it lies at an altitude of 900m (3,000ft) on the slopes of the sacred volcano Gunung Agung. The Balinese have always regarded their mountains as holy, but no one quite knows when exactly the first temple was erected on the abode of the gods. What is certain is that the temples can be traced back to the 11th century.

A TRIO OF TEMPLES

One of the three most important temple complexes is ★★ **Pura Panataran Agung**, which is dedicated to Sanghyang Widhi Wasa in his incarnation as Shiva. This does not prevent the Balinese from worshipping the trinity of Shiva, Brahma and Vishnu in the main courtyard. This one temple consists of some 60 individual edifices spread across seven ascending terraces.

To the east lies the second of the three main complexes, the **Pura Kiduling Kreteng**, which is dedicated to Brahma and maintained by the Bangli royal family. Finally, to the west, lies the third of the 'trinity' of temples, the **Pura Batu Madeg**, which is dedicated to Vishnu. A staircase

Pre-Hindu worship
There is evidence that a temple has stood at the Pura Besakih site since the 11th century. Pre-Hindu rituals are believed to have taken place here. From the late 15th century, it became an ancestral shrine for the powerful Gelgel-Klungkung dynasty, whose descendants maintain the Shiva complex to this day.

In the festive mood

flanked by figures from the Mahabharata leads to the split gate, through which pilgrims can enter the first temple courtyard of the Pura Panataran Agung. Only Hindus are allowed in, so for other visitors there is a staircase which circumvents the temple and gives a good view of the main courtyard. The latter contains the shrines of the trinity, frequently covered with brightly coloured cloths.

In the northeast corner of the temple complex is a little stall offering snacks, and providing the best vantage point of the landscape and beauty of this sacred and dignified place.

Star Attraction

● **Pura Panataran Agung**

Below: produce at Pura Besakih
Bottom: a gathering of devotees

THE EKADASA RUDRA

Pura Besakih is the setting for a highly important ritual. Once every century, the Ekadasa Rudra, the greatest of Balinese sacrifices, is performed to purify the entire universe. During the years of colonial rule (after the 16th century), the sacrifice was not observed. At the beginning of the 1960s, however, the Balinese believe that the gods suddenly showed their displeasure by sending a series of poor harvests and political unrest upon the island.

The local priests were consulted and it seemed that the only way to put a stop to the island's misfortunes was to placate the gods with sacrificial offerings. And so, in February 1963, preparations for the Ekadasa Rudra began. Suddenly, a glow of fire shone from the crater and Gunung Agung – which hadn't erupted for more than a century and was considered extinct – began to rumble. A priestess interpreted the ashes of the volcano as a sacred portent, and the people continued with their festival arrangements.

THE VOLCANO ERUPTS

However, soon after the sacrifice on March 8, Gunung Agung erupted with unimaginable force. Large parts of eastern Bali were destroyed by the streams of lava, and more than 2,000 people were killed. As if by a miracle, however, the streams of lava split in two before they reached Pura Besakih

Map on pages 40–41

Scenic trek
South of Besakih, near Rendang, turn toward Putung for an excellent vantage point across rice terraces and coconut groves, over the ocean to Nusa Penida island. A path links Putung to Manggis village, through *salak* plantations and rice fields, making an excellent two-hour downhill trek.

Below: restaurant at Putung
Bottom: mountain view

and flowed past the sanctuary, leaving it undamaged. To most Balinese the eruption did not occur by chance, but was chastisement for having offended the gods. According to the Balinese *Saka* calendar, the islanders were not in fact supposed to celebrate the Ekadasa Rudra until March 1979.

When that auspicious day finally came, the sacrifice was held without incident: the gods accepted the offerings and more than a million Balinese came to Gunung Agung to pay their respects to the mountain. The entire festival lasted almost two months.

Candidasa Option

If you have had enough of sightseeing for the day, return by the same route via Klungkung. Otherwise, make a picturesque, albeit time-consuming detour, via **Selat** and **Putung**, to the coast at Candidasa. With stops, it should take about two hours to reach Candidasa, where you should spend the night. To follow this route, take the side turning to the left near the restaurant by the car park. The road leads through *salak* plantations, little villages and magnificent rice terraces.

In Candidasa

The route continues through Bungaya and Prasi, and eventually arrives in ★ **Candidasa**. It was not until the early 1980s that this little fishing village on a lovely bay began its transformation into a seaside resort, with the aim of attracting tourists away from the beaches at Kuta and Sanur. The first visitors to arrive were backpackers, but the quality of accommodation was soon improved to meet more demanding tastes.

Today, there is hardly an empty plot of land along the beach – or rather, what is left of it. Dynamite fishing destroyed the protective coral reefs, and nature took its revenge by washing away the sand. For several years, attempts were made to prevent this erosion by means of concrete walls. Some hotels offer artificial alternatives by constructing new swimming pools.

Apart from the beach, Candidasa is still a pretty place with some attractive hotels and good fish restaurants. It remains a good base from which to explore the east coast *(see page 67)*.

Serious students of culture should visit Ibu Gedong's **Gandhian Ashram** Started in the 1970s as a self-sufficient community based on Gandhian principles, the *ashram* once was the only structure along this isolated beach. The founder, Gedong Bagoes Oka, has worked to support the environment and help young people learn useful trades. Bungalows for rent (tel: 0363-41108) provide simple accommodation for volunteers.

PADANG BAI

If you prefer not to continue along the eastern route to Singaraja, return to the south along the main road through Klungkung. The little village of ★ **Padang Bai**, which lies on a beautiful bay, boasts the island's only natural harbour. For many years it provided the only direct sea link with Lombok. Today, a ferry still leaves here for the neighbouring island three times daily, although fast boats also leave from Benoa Harbour in the south. Inter-island ferries and passenger ships also embark here on island-hopping itineraries to the eastward chain of islands of Nusa Tenggara, stretching from Lombok to West Timor.

Below: the coast at Candidasa
Below: local baby snapper

Map on pages 40–41

War of gods

East of Candidasa lies Bugbug, a Bali Aga (Old Balinese) village in structure. Here, once every two years on the full moon of the fourth Balinese month (October), the War of the Gods or Perang Dewa occurs on a hilltop. Four surrounding villages gather and hang offerings of suckling pig in the trees. They bring statues of their gods to battle one another.

Padang Bai is enclosed by white sand coves and turquoise sea. A few *losmen* (guesthouses) and a fine beach make this a great stop over. The area's history is closely connected with the great priest Empu Kuturan, who arrived in the 11th century, the father of village organization and reform.

GOA LAWAH

About 3km (2 miles) past Padang Bai, you will come to ★ **Goa Lawah**, the 'Bat Cave' temple dedicated to the spirits of the underworld. The temple itself is of little artistic interest, although its origins can be traced back to the 11th century. Nonetheless, it is one of the royal temples and is regarded as the counterpart to Pura Besakih, the temple of heaven.

Legend has it that the cave leads all the way back to Besakih, and may even continue to an underground river that supposedly comes up at Pura Goa, within the Besakih complex. The main attraction at Goa Lawah is the colony of bats – thousands of them – which seem to be permanently glued to the walls of the cave. Their presence accounts for the sweetish odour and the droppings which cover the temple shrines.

The temple is held to be ruled by two snakes, Basuki and Antaboga – who, providing they like bats, will never go hungry.

Local women with bamboo

KUSUMBA

On the other side of the road at ★ **Kusamba** is a black lava beach, a relic of the last eruption of Gunung Agung. Colourful *prahu* (outriggers) line the shores of this fishing village. Rows of brown, thatched huts emerge from the sand – small factories for making salt. The villagers gather wet sand from the sea, spreading it along sand banks on the beach. After drying, the sand is dumped into large bins in the huts. Slowly, water with a high salt content drains through the sands. The residue is poured into bamboo troughs to evaporate in the sun, leaving salt crystals.

The process takes two days in good weather, yielding 5 kilograms (11 lbs) of salt. The best time of day to visit this particular area is at sunset, when the beach is bathed in a magical light and the local inhabitants gather round to chat.

Below: extracting salt at Kusamba
Bottom: Amlapura sunset

EXCURSIONS FROM CANDIDASA

AMLAPURA

Taking the road heading northeast out of Candidasa, you will arrive at **Amlapura**, the main town of the Karangasem regency. After the disintegration of the rulers of the Gelgel/Klungkung dynasties, **Karangasem** developed during the 17th and 18th centuries into the most powerful principality on the island. Apart from governing Bali, its rajas also partly ruled over neighbouring Lombok.

The Golden Age of Karangasem continued when the Dutch occupied the island. Like the Raja of Gianyar, the Raja of Karangasem made a treaty with the colonial forces. Whilst the palaces of Badung and Klungkung were laid to ashes, the local raja was able to retain not only his title but also some of his power.

This was the reason why the royal family was able to maintain its elaborate court and indulge in its love of lavish water palaces until World War II. However, these magnificent relics from the most glittering period of the region's history became victims of natural catastrophe when Gunung Agung erupted in 1963 *(see page 63)*.

Map on pages 40–41

Dutch style
One of several *bale* (pavilions) found at the Puri Kanginan is the Bale Maskerdam, named after Amsterdam in the Netherlands. Inside this "Amsterdam Hall" are several rooms, including a royal bedroom decorated with furniture presented by the Dutch royal family of the time. A treaty between the Raja of Karangasem and the Dutch allowed the regency to survive long after other Balinese kingdoms had fallen to Dutch rule.

Chess mates in Ujung

Puri Kanginan

Until Gunung Agung volcano erupted, the town of Amlapura bore the same name as the province, which was named after the ancient kingdom of Karangasem. After the catastrophe, as an optimistic indication of its new beginning, the town received its new name.

The ★★ **Puri Kanginan**, the palace where the last raja was born, has definitely seen better days, but when it was built at the beginning of the 20th century it was considered to be one of the most magnificent palaces on the entire island. The various *bale* (pavilions) of the palace are grouped around an artificial lake and display an interesting hotchpotch of styles, linking Balinese, European and Chinese elements.

Taman Ujung

Four kilometres (3 miles) southeast of the provincial capital lies the fishing village of Ujung. The ruins of the water palace, **Taman Ujung**, which dates back to 1919, were damaged during the volcanic catastrophe of 1963.

The ruins are in danger of being swallowed up by the surrounding vegetation, but you can still sense the former grandeur and magnificence of the complex. With a little imagination it is easy to picture the water-loving raja bathing in his pleasure palace, surrounded by his companions. There are plans to renovate the buildings.

Taman Tirthagangga

During the 1940s, as a contrast to his palace by the sea, the last raja built another water palace, ★ **Taman Tirthagangga**, on the slopes of Gunung Agung, 6km (4 miles) northwest of Amlapura. With its mixture of Balinese, Chinese and European architectural elements, the water park was acclaimed as a marvel of engineering at the time. Although parts of the 'Ganges Water Garden', were damaged by the eruption of Gunung Agung in 1963, the pools and fountains are still intact. Some of them have been restored, and one of the pools has been transformed into a public bathing pool. It is quiet for most of the day, but comes alive with locals during the late afternoon and on weekends.

A dip in the cool spring water, fed by mountain streams and spouting out of fountains and stone animals, provides welcome relief from the heat before lunch in the palace restaurant. Long walks across the fields provide a good opportunity to study the irrigation structures.

Star Attractions
- **Puri Kanginan**
- **Tenganan**

TENGANAN

★★ **Tenganan**, which lies in the hills 3km (2 miles) north of Candidasa, is one of the few villages in Bali where the culture of the Bali Aga, the Old Balinese, has been preserved. Visitors without their own transport will be met on the approach road by motorbike taxis.

The alternative is to take a scenic three-hour walk to the village, but be forewarned that only hardy walkers should attempt this. The road surface is very uneven in places, and walkers face a fair amount of uphill and downhill climbing. The breathtaking views more than compensate for the exertion. The path begins opposite the Ida Homestay in the centre of town.

The Tenganan region, covering an area of 350 hectares (865 acres), is divided into five districts

Below: a colourful cock bred for fighting
Bottom: masks in Tenganan

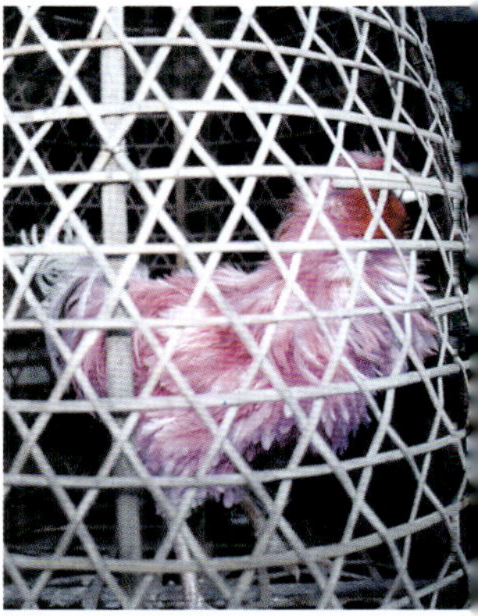

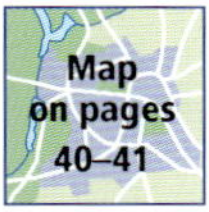

and has a population of about 3,500. The true Bali Aga live in the village of Tenganan Pegeringsingan, whose population has remained constant at about 300 for many years.

Until the 1970s, Tenganan was a closed society, visited only by the occasional ethnologist. An entrance fee is now charged, a sign that times have changed. Even at a distance, Tenganan looks different from other Balinese villages. It is surrounded by a wall and can be entered only through one of four gates. The homesteads are lined up along the village road, which leads up the mountain. In the middle are the community rooms and the assembly pavilions.

The people of Tenganan are proud of their lineage, which they trace back to the god Indra. They have never adopted the caste system favoured by the other islanders, and live according to the ancient traditions of the Bali Aga.

Below: ikat *for sale, Tenganan*
Bottom: lontar *books*

Village Traditions and Rituals

The village men of Tenganan traditionally own land, letting their possessions work for them and banking the profits, which is enough to guarantee an almost carefree life.

Each member of the village community must submit him- or herself to the traditional rules of society. From an early age, the children become

members of boys' or girls' associations, through which they learn the basic precepts of the Bali Aga community. The strictest rule is endogamy, i.e. marriage only within the village community. Anyone taking a partner outside the village boundaries must live in the Street of Exiles at the far end of the village or even leave the village entirely. This rule keeps the land within the community. However, it has also led to fertility problems and decreasing numbers of Tenganese.

Tenganan village is full of unusual customs and practices. During certain rituals, young women and men dressed in *geringsing (see below)* dance to traditional music. At the annual Usaba Sambah festival in June/July, young girls ride wooden ferris wheels propelled by foot power. During the festival, the village men fight the *makare*, using thorny leaves to ritually draw blood as sacrifice.

Healing fabrics
The sacred *geringsing* fabrics of Tenganan village are known for their protective powers and their ability to cure illnesses. Its name may come from the words *gering* (ill) and *sing* (not), although *geringsing* itself means 'speckled', which is an appropriate description of these shimmering textiles.

IKAT WEAVING AND *LONTAR*

Also world-famous is Tenganan's double *ikat* weaving technique. It is a highly complex procedure in which both warp and weft threads are dyed before the weaving process begins. The women who sit at the looms need a great deal of patience in order to fit the patterns together. Some of the cloths, reserved for ritual purposes, are the result of years of work. It's no wonder that the next generation of weavers is in short supply.

The cloths – called *geringsing* and known for their healing and magical properties – are coveted items in Bali, and collectors are willing to pay high prices for these precious fabrics. In the village souvenir shops, however, you will often find inferior quality fabrics on sale at lower prices.

Another Balinese tradition which has survived in Tenganan is *lontar* books. This involves etching the leaves of the lontar palm with Old Balinese texts and illustrations from the great Hindu epics. The leaves are then cut into narrow pages, pressed between two wooden covers and bound with twine. The task is undertaken by men, who inscribe the characters and pictures onto leaves previously soaked in a bath of plant extracts.

Ikat *weaving*

Map on pages 40–41

Coastal beauty
Stunning valley and bay views along the harsh and arid northeast lie around every bend of the road which hugs the coastline. The challenging drive and sparse population make it all the more attractive.

Below: along the north coast
Bottom: on the road to Amed

7: Along the Northeastern Coast

Candidasa – Amed – Tulamben – Kubutambahan – Singaraja – Lovina Beach

Once visitors have been to the island's interior, they are usually inspired to explore further north. This route, which follows the sometimes wild and arid coast of eastern Bali to the north of the island, takes you to undeveloped and often charming places. Kubutambahan boasts a North Balinese temple which is markedly different from all the other temples on the island. Singaraja is the hub of the north, and the beaches of Lovina form the tourist centre on the north coast.

The Road to Amed

The route, starting from Candidasa and heading around on the east coast as far as Lovina Beach, covers a distance of 160km (100 miles). Over the centuries, the volcanic forces of fire and the power of water have created a unique and inaccessible coastal landscape around Gunung Seraya (1,175m/3,855ft), which is as yet largely unknown to most tourists.

If you decide to take this route, the section from Ujung around the coast to Amed is especially tricky: be prepared to negotiate some 50 hair-raising kilometres (30 miles) along narrow and, in places, badly maintained roads with many sharp bends. This section of the journey alone will take up to two hours.

Furthermore, if it has rained hard, some of the streams that must be crossed along the route will have turned into miniature rivers, representing an insurmountable obstacle, even with a four-wheel drive vehicle. Less adventurous drivers should take the shorter 135km (84 miles) route from Candidasa via Amlapura, northwest through Taman Tirthagangga *(see page 68)*.

Rice-Terraced Landscape

Whether it is bright and sunny or rainy and gloomy, the trip through the ★★ **rice-terrace**

landscape between Candidasa and Amlapura is one of remarkable scenic beauty. The harsh tropical weather of Bali has turned into fertile soil some of the streams of lava which flowed across the countryside southeast of Karangasem during the last eruption of Gunung Agung.

Most people will want to make frequent photography stops or go for short walks to examine more closely the skilled architecture of the rice terraces. One stop, in any case, is essential. As you drive into Amlapura, stop at the Pertamina petrol station on the east side of the road.

Star Attraction
- Rice terraces between Candidasa and Amlapura

Below: rice terrace landscape
Bottom: outriggers, a typical coastal feature

SCENIC STOPS

Just before the royal palace in **Amlapura** *(see page 68)* is a turning southeast leading to Ujung. After you have passed the **Taman Ujung** water palace *(see also page 68)*, the paddy fields peter out and give way to less fertile upland. Maize and vegetables are interspersed with the occasional vines, and village life reflects the meagre natural resources of the area.

The volcanic debris, deposited on the eastern coast of the island, has created a semicircular protuberance where the deeply cleft slopes of the mountain plunge down to the sea to form a succession of bays, fringed by a line of brightly painted *prahus* (fishing outriggers). Shortly before

Map on pages 40–41

> ***Liberty* wreck**
> The American warship, USS *Liberty* was torpedoed by a Japanese submarine in 1942, and ran aground at Tulamben. In 1963, Gunung Agung's eruption pushed the vessel off the beach, splitting the hull. Today, the site of the shipwreck is Bali's most-visited dive site.

Below: scuba diving equipment
Bottom: lontar palm frond

you reach the fishing village of **Amed**, you will come to **Lipah Beach** before continuing the journey to **Culik**. Here you should turn to the north.

The most tiring part of the journey is now over, and the route continues along a well maintained road through landscape interspersed with outcrops of rock. At **Tulamben**, the scenery changes drastically to dry hills covered with scrub. This beach is a favourite with water sports enthusiasts. Apart from the main pastimes of diving and snorkelling, there is little else of interest here.

Northeast Coastal Road

The northeastern coast road continues through the sparsely populated, austere, coastal lowlands. It seems surprising that a tropical island like Bali should possess such an arid region. Scrubland gives way to lontar palm trees, with the occasional field of dry crops such as maize, soy beans and peanuts. The road crosses a number of dried-out watercourses and is bounded by stone walls on which a few cactuses grow.

During the monsoon season, the lava gullies fill with streams of water from the northern flank of Gunung Agung. Depending on the weather and time of day, the volcano rises majestically above the countryside or disappears behind a curtain of clouds. A popular stopover is Sambirenteng, where the Alam Anda Bungalows provide a congenial overnight stay *(see page 125)*.

As you head towards **Air Sanih**, the northern foothills of Gunung Penulisan are covered with thick vegetation. The spring water pool on the north side of the road provides an opportunity for a refreshing swim. Simple accommodation and a restaurant are available here.

Kubutambahan's Attractions

Kubutambahan, the next stop, is the nearest you will get to the northern tip of the island. In the centre of the village, on the right-hand side of the street, stands the ★**Pura Meduwe Karang**. Spread across three terraces, the temple is very different in style from those found in southern Bali. As well as the *Trimurti* (Brahma, Vishnu and Shiva), the 'Lord of the Fields' is worshipped here. He is the masculine equivalent of the rice goddess Dewi Sri, and watches over the coffee and maize crops in the region.

The temple also has its army of guardians in the form of young boys, who will greet you on the steps leading up to the first terrace, to guide you to the famous motif of the lotus bicycle on the northern perimeter wall. The bicycle's wheel and cog are depicted as stone flowers, while a real frangipani blossom often adorns the carved ear of the cyclist, said to be a rendition of W.O.J. Nieuwenkamp, a Dutch archaeologist who travelled around the island on a bicycle at the turn of the century. Other reliefs depict a Legong dancer and rural scenes like that of a farmer ploughing a field.

PURA BEJI

About 8km (5 miles) before Singaraja, in the village of **Sangsit**, is the **Pura Beji**. Built in the 15th century and dedicated to the rice goddess Dewi Sri, this temple is adorned with numerous *naga* (serpents), which are symbols of fertility. The local *subak*, the association which manages the water needed to irrigate the rice fields, is responsible for the upkeep of this temple.

Below and bottom: details of the Pura Meduwe Karang

Map on pages 40–41

> **Historic library**
> Gedung Kirtya Library on Singaraja's Jalan Veteran houses almost 3,000 books on *lontar* palm leaves, recording the island's history, literature, legends and religion. These are the oldest documents on the island, important for scientific research rather than of interest to visitors (open 7am–3pm Monday–Thursday, until noon Friday).

Singaraja

The route continues to ★ **Singaraja**. With a population of some 30,000 inhabitants, this town is the commercial centre of the north as well as the administrative capital of the district of Buleleng. The town was of great importance in the late 19th century when Bali was under Dutch colonial rule, and until 1945 it was the capital of Bali.

Today, Singaraja has lost its political and economic significance. Singaraja is worth exploring at night. After dark the streets fill with life, with the **night market** turning into a centre of activity and the aroma of freshly grilled satay wafting around the stalls.

Lovina Beach

Lovina Beach

The route continues along the main road towards Gilimanuk, crosses the fertile coastal plain and, after another 10km (6 miles), reaches **Lovina Beach**. Several villages form the hub of a number of tourist enclaves which are strung out along the coast. The black lava beaches and their murky waters can't be compared with those in the south of the island, but the region is ideal for visitors in search of peace and relaxation.

There is some good snorkelling on the offshore reef, but those who prefer to stay dry can take a boat trip to see the dolphins which swim along the coast. The mountain scenery in the vicinity will encourage you to explore the area on foot, while the beach is ideal for strolling. There are numerous *losmen* (guesthouses) and mid-range hotels and resorts for visitors planning a longer stay.

Excursions from Lovina

Ahe Road to Lake Bratan

The two-hour drive from Lovina to Lake Bratan along a winding, minor road will pass through dramatically beautiful mountain scenery. But first, make a stop to visit the ★★ **Brahma Vihara Monastery**. From Lovina, turn off towards Banjar just before Seririt. The monastery is situated high up on a hill just south of Banjar and has lovely views.

Inhabited by a single Buddhist monk, the complex is spread out across a terrace around a lotus pond. The paintings on the wall of the main hall relate episodes from the life of Buddha, worshipped by Bali's Chinese population.

Return to the coastal road and continue till you reach Seririt, where a turn south leads to Pupuan and Denpasar. A few kilometres further on, in the village of Mayong, take the road signposted to Munduk. Passing between rice fields, the road slowly climbs into the mountains, offering breathtaking views through the steep valleys cutting through the cloud-covered volcanoes.

The coast gradually retreats and, between Kayuputih and Munduk, the narrow road meanders between dense hedges of coffee, cocoa and vanilla plantations growing in the shade of a forest of lofty clove trees. Shortly after entering the village of **Munduk**, you may choose to break your journey at the Puri Lumbung Bungalow complex and spend the night *(see page 125)*.

A TRIO OF LAKES

Lake Tamblingan and **Lake Buyan** lie a short distance further, close together on the west side below the road. Because of the higher altitude,

Star Attraction
- **Brahma Vihara Monastery**

Below: Brahma Vihara Monastery
Bottom: Buddha detail

Map on pages 40–41

Highland gardens
West of the market in Candi Kuning is the Kebun Eka Raya Botanical Gardens. Explore the grounds of this sprawling, tropical 'alpine' forest park of pine trees and hiking trails, and visit the orchid and cactus greenhouses. The whole area is very unlike the rest of Bali.

temperatures are much lower here than the coast, giving the whole area an alpine feel. You will shortly come to the main road linking the north and south of the island, which runs along the west bank of ★★ **Lake Bratan**. Nestling amongst the cloud-covered forests, this mysterious lake is said to be the home of Dewi Danu, the goddess of the lake. She is worshipped in the spectacularly located ★★ **Pura Ulun Danu**, where two shrines seem to rise from the waters. Set against beautifully landscaped gardens, the temple was built in 1633 by the Raja of Mengwi.

BEDUGUL

On the lake is **Bedugul**, a small town which has given its name to this entire mountain lake area, with its clear, crisp air, long-used as a weekend retreat by the Balinese. Nearby **Candi Kuning** boasts a wonderfully colourful spice, fruit and orchid market, which will leave a vivid impression of the cornucopia of tropical flora in Bali. For those wishing to spend a night here, Kalaspa Health Retreat offers cosy lakeview rooms *(see page 123)*.

Bottom: Pura Ulun Danu

MENJANGAN ISLAND

Also known as Deer Island, ★ **Menjangan** is an arid island off the northwest coast of Bali. It forms part of the **Bali Barat National Park** *(see page 115)* and is a popular destination for diving and snorkelling enthusiasts. The island is uninhabited except for the Java Deer, and overnight stays are prohibited by the national park authorities.

You can book an organised day trip in Lovina through one of the diving operators *(see page 114)*. Alternatively, your hotel in Lovina may also arrange similar excursions. Don't forget your passport, as all visitors to the national park have to be registered.

If you are exploring the north coast of Bali and want to stop for a night or two, turn off to the right a few kilometres after the Pulaki Temple in Pemuteran. The signs to Pondok Sari will lead you to the pretty bungalow complex *(see pages 124–5)*.

8: To the North Coast via Gunung Batur

Map on pages 40–41

Sidan – Bangli – Penelokan – Gunung Batur – Pura Jagaraga – Singaraja – Lovina

The journey to the north offers a chance to see yet more Balinese temples, as well as experience the island's spectacular scenery. An alternative to the route described here would be to follow the shorter route via Lake Bratan *(see page 78)*. Allow sufficient time to visit the less frequented temples and for the relatively easy ascent of Gunung Batur. Toya Bungkah is a convenient starting point for the Gunung Batur, while Lovina makes a good base for a restful holiday.

If you follow the main road to Klungkung, the turning to Bangli and Kintamani lies on your left as you drive through the village of Peteluan, a few kilometres east of the regional capital of Gianyar. Traffic conditions are less crowded here than on the east of the island, and your enjoyment will increase as you approach the highlands.

Star Attractions
- Lake Bratan
- Pura Ulun Danu

Below: Pura Dalem Sidan
Bottom: rural idyll near Sidan

Pura Dalem Sidan

After about 2 km (1 mile) you will come to the ★**Pura Dalem Sidan**, the 'Temple of the Dead'. The complex lies on a right-hand bend and presents a spectacular sight. The temple architecture

Map on pages 40–41

recalls that of northern Bali, and the elaborate decorations reveal a remarkable attention to detail.

Dramatic portraits of Rangda with long, flame-like tongues adorn the split gate. In front of the external perimeter wall are a number of elaborate sculptures of assorted fabulous creatures and monsters, such as the fat demon resting his arm on the sole of his foot.

The most important architectural element of the temple is the magnificent covered gate, which is surrounded by a stone border and appears to stand in the midst of a ring of fire. Its harmonious *candi* shape recalls that of Mount Mahameru *(see page 97)*. The gate is flanked by two guardian figures of Rangda and a sculpture of the Durga, which has just conquered the buffalo demon in human form. Balinese temples of the dead are always dedicated to Durga and Shiva *(see page 95)*.

Royal farmers
Now an agricultural area growing sweet potatoes, peanuts, corn and spices, Bangli was the capital of a kingdom descended from the early Gelgel dynasty.

Below and bottom: banyan tree and kulkul *tower at the Pura Kehen*

Bangli

Continuing through the fertile paddy fields and a succession of apparently prosperous villages, the road climbs steadily towards **Bangli**. This neat and tidy capital of the administrative region of the same name was once the centre of the Kingdom of Bangli and has managed to retain its charming rural atmosphere. Its entrance is marked by a *kulkul* drum tower.

Pura Kehen

The ★★ **Pura Kehen** is the religious heart of the town's many temples. It lies on the northern edge of the built-up area, to the east of the main road to Kintamani. This 'Temple of the Treasury' is one of the largest religious complexes on Bali. The first courtyard, whose origins can be traced back to the 11th century, was constructed as a symbol of Mount Mahameru, the 'world mountain' *(see page 97)*. It contains an enormous banyan tree and a *kulkul* tower. An attractively decorated *kori agung* (covered gate), leads through to the first courtyard, while the *candi bentar* (split gate) serves as entrance to the second.

Look out for the plates adorning the terrace wall leading to the *jeroan* (third courtyard). The Chinese porcelain used to decorate the temple was considered very valuable as it was imported from abroad: some plates have been damaged or stolen and subsequently replaced so try spotting these.

Star Attraction
● Pura Kehen

The Three Worlds

The 11-tiered *meru* is dedicated to Shiva and contains the temple treasures. It stands on the back of the tortoise Bedawang, who is entwined by two *naga* (mythological snakes). The construction provides an analogy of the Balinese conception of the universe, with the tortoise representing the Underworld, the main body of the shrine the Middle World, and the 11-tiered pagoda roof the Upper World. The *padmasana* (lotus throne) is an impressive piece of work with its fine representations of various deities. During temple festivals, the throne is reserved as the seat of honour for the guests from the Upper World.

Below: local children
Bottom: Temple of the Treasury

To Gunung Batur

The next section of the road is well maintained but relatively little used. After 25km (16 miles), the road winds uphill towards Batur, and paddy fields gradually give way to bamboo groves and

Map on pages 40–41

Trunyan village
This Bali Aga village near Lake Batur, accessible only by boat or a trek, is well known, but a visit is not recommended. The people are known to 'beg'aggresively, and some tourists have had to pay money in order to be allowed to leave the village.

vegetable and clove plantations. The vegetation is less luxuriant as the climate is cooler here. Driving through the villages you will also be reminded that conditions here are harsher than in the lowlands, as the settlements are more scattered.

If visibility is good, as you enter ★★ **Penelokan** ('Place of the View'), you will have a breathtaking view of ★ **Gunung Batur** (1,717m/5,633ft), revered by the Balinese as the second most holy mountain on the island. The slopes of this still active volcano are covered by extensive fields of black lava, which continue far down into the massive caldera. The basin-shaped valley, formed millions of years ago, contains Gunung Batur itself and the lake of the same name. On the southeastern shore of the lake stands Gunung Abang (2,153m/7,064ft), whose summit forms the highest point of the cauldron.

Toya Bungkah

Below: Toya Bungkah

Visitors wishing to climb Gunung Batur should drive down to **Toya Bungkah**, about half an hour further on. The village lies on the western shore of the lake, and along the way the route is dotted with outcrops of lava left during the volcano's last eruption in 1963. Several hotels provide a comfortable alternative to the simple *losmen* (guesthouses) in the village. You may be tempted to go for a swim in the hot springs *(air panas)*, especially on your return from Gunung Batur. However, there are no changing facilities here.

On the opposite shore is the village of **Trunyan**. Like Tenganan *(see page 69)*, the Bali Aga, or the original pre-Hindu Balinese people of Trunyan, rejected the changes brought by the Majapahit invaders in the 14th century. The villagers have kept their own animist customs, including the practice of leaving the dead in open pits to decompose, oddly with no accompanying stench.

Trekking up Batur

Get up very early the next day – 4am at the latest – if you want to witness dawn on the summit of

Gunung Batur. The path is clearly marked but you will need a guide and stout shoes, as the upper slopes consist of sharp-edged lava stones and dust. Trekkers who are reasonably fit will need between four and five hours, including a leisurely pause for breakfast, to get to the summit and back. If it is raining, even experienced walkers should think carefully before setting out as the path will be slippery and possibly even hazardous. Under such conditions, in any case, the sunrise will be a washout.

Star Attractions
- Penelokan
- Pura Tegeh Koripan

PURA TEGEH KORIPAN

Back in Penelokan, continue along the rim of the crater through Kintamani to **Penulisan**, where more than 300 steps lead up to the highest temple on the island. The ★★ **Pura Tegeh Koripan** on Gunung Penulisan (1,745m/5,725ft) consists of two simple courtyards which are not adorned with the usual *meru* (pagoda-like shrines). Instead there are numerous pavilions housing a large collection of stone sculptures. They represent various deities, including two well-preserved portraits of Ganesh, as well as former rulers. In some cases, the items can be traced back more than 1,000 years.

The origin, age and purpose of some sculptures have not yet been determined. Some bear the *linga-yoni* motifs which symbolise the duality of male and female characteristics. The temple affords a

Below and bottom: Gunung Batur guide and panorama

Map on pages 40–41

Musical Sawan

Sawan village is an important production centre for *gamelan* instruments *(see page 105)*. You can see brass gongs being cast, and the wooden frames carved by master craftsmen. Sawan is also known for its troupe of very accomplished dancers.

Below: carved plane relief at Pura Jagaraga
Bottom: sculpture detail

fine view of the two sacred mountains, Gunung Agung and Gunung Batur. On a clear day you can even see as far as Gunung Rinjani on Lombok.

Pura Tegeh Koripan also marks the highest point on the road, which then winds its way down through cloud-covered pine forests over a distance of 32km (20 miles) back to Singaraja. Rushing torrents filled by the frequent mountain rains accompany the road on its way. As the route continues away from the summit, it offers glimpses of the coast once again. The horizon, bathed in light, forms a stark contrast to the cloudy skies above the mountains.

Pura Jagaraga

The route continues westwards from Kubutambahan, passing the Pura Meduwe Karang *(see page 74)*. Just before the village of Sangsit, take the south fork to **Sawan**.

Halfway along this stretch is the ★**Pura Jagaraga**. The sculpted shapes and wealth of decorations make this temple one of the masterpieces of North Balinese religious architecture. The gate, which is unusually broad and therefore appears out of proportion, and the walls of this 'Temple of the Underworld' *(pura dalem)* are covered with ornamental detail best described as Balinese baroque. The carved stone figures seem to caricature certain details of physiognomy, with goggle-eyed demons and Rangdas with pendulous breasts and elongated fingers looking as if they had just stepped out of a cartoon.

Even more astounding are the reliefs on either side of the exterior wall. The central characters are white foreigners who represent a threat to the islanders. Expect to see scenes like those of two Europeans in a Model T Ford being held up by bandits, flying aces in aircraft plunging into the sea, and a Dutch steamer signalling an SOS when it is suddenly attacked by sea monsters. The scenes are a thought-provoking allegory of the Balinese fears of the world of the white colonials.

Continue to Lovina Beach where overnight accommodation can be found *(see page 124)*.

9: The Rice Terraces of Pupuan

Lovina Beach – Pupuan Belimbing – Antosari – South Bali

Map on pages 40–41

The route via Pupuan is one of the most attractive of the roads that link the south and the north of the island. The trip from Lovina Beach through the thinly populated western interior of Bali to Denpasar is about 100km (60 miles). Because of the area's relative isolation, the luxuriance of the tropical vegetation and the fertility of the island become all the more impressive. The route also passes through Bali's only grape-growing area, which lies near Lovina on the fertile coastal strip.

Star Attractions (overleaf)
- Views on the road to Pupuan
- Belimbing

Worthwhile Detours

The main coast road in the direction of Gilimanuk branches off in Seririt towards Pupuan and Denpasar. If you wish to bathe in the nearby hot springs, ★ **Air Panes** (the route is signposted; open daily 9am-6pm), continue through Tangguwesia and rejoin the main route at Pengastulan. From Busungbiyu, the scenery becomes progressively more dramatic.

You can also make a detour to see the **Brahma Vihara** monastery *(see page 75)*. In this case, take the turning to Banjar just before entering Seririt. The monastery is situated just south of the village.

Below: grapes from Lovina
Bottom: rice terraces on the road to Pupuan

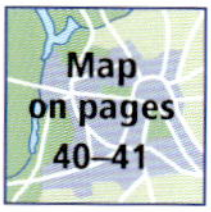

Plentiful palms
To the uninitiated, a palm tree is a tall thing with fringed leaves and coconuts. In Indonesia alone, there are over 480 species of the palm tree. Palm trees yield, among other things – palm sugar, beverages, fruit, betel nuts, oil, wax, building materials, tools and instruments, and fibres like coir, which are made into mats and baskets.

Copra production

PUPUAN

Continuing along the road to **Pupuan**, the route is accompanied by a series of breathtaking ★★ **views**. Many visitors park their cars at the side of the road and get out to take a short walk or photograph the scenery. The steeply terraced rice fields are overwhelmingly beautiful as they plunge down the hillside in places like precipitous canyons.

You can clearly make out the course taken by the water as it flows along rivers or lined canals, passing from the higher to the lower terraces. The Balinese genius is evident in these masterpieces of engineering. On the upper slopes the rice terraces give way to *salak*, banana and clove plantations. South of Pupuan, the road gradually descends before winding westwards across the western foothills of Gunung Batukau. The volcano's summit is usually covered in clouds during the afternoon as you drive past the coffee and coconut plantations.

Half-way between Pupuan and Antosari, ★★ **Belimbing** village overlooks steep, breathtaking rice paddy vistas in the shadow of Gunung Batukau mountain. Belimbing Kafe is operated by the Woworuntu family, of Sanur's Batujimbar Café fame. Behind the café at Cempaka Belimbing, two clusters of villas – one overlooking the mountain, one overlooking rice fields and surrounding a swimming pool – offer delightful overnight accommodation.

COCONUT PALMS

By the roadside you will notice collection points for copra, which come from the plentiful palm trees in the area. The shelled coconuts are transported to Java, where the flesh is extracted and used as an ingredient in the production of traditional Indonesian cosmetics. The shells are taken to Tabanan, where they are processed into fibrous mats and used as roofing material.

In Antosari the road rejoins the main route to Denpasar and the more populated tourist centres of the south coast.

Lombok

Map below

The neighbouring island of Lombok lies to the east of Bali, across the Strait of Lombok. Passing through this narrow stretch of ocean (35km/22 miles wide and 300m/984ft deep) is the famous Wallace Line *(see page 8)*. The island also belongs to the Lesser Sundas group, and covers an area of 4,600sq km (1,776sq miles). The geographical contrasts between the north and south of the island are remarkable. Surrounding Gunung Rinjani, one of the highest mountains in Indonesia (3,726m/12,224ft), the northern half of the island is crossed by a chain of mountains largely cloaked with impenetrable teak forests.

Outrigger on Sengiggi Beach

THE ENVIRONMENT

The agriculturally useful land in Lombok lies in the highlands, and the adjoining fertile areas run from the more densely populated western region

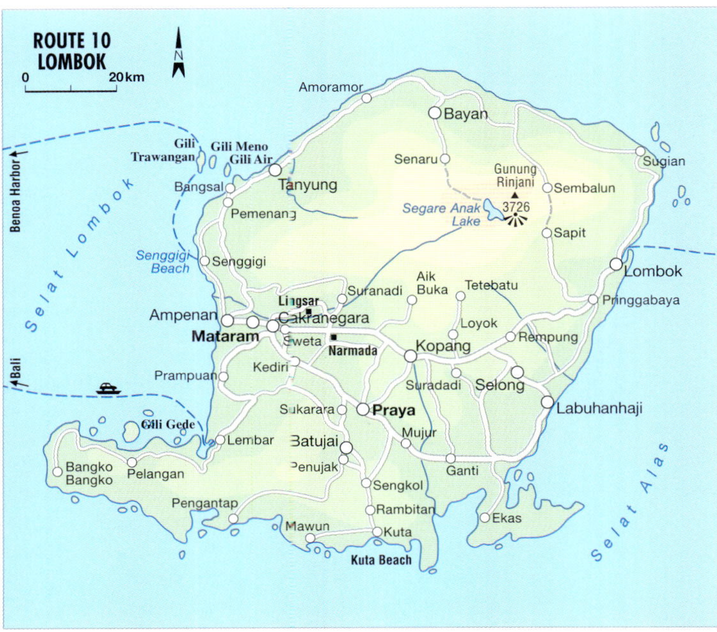

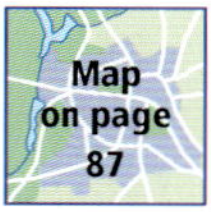

towards the east. The arid coastal lowlands are covered with savannah-like vegetation. There is no industry on the island, and conditions for rice farming are less favourable than on Bali as the climate is drier. The main agricultural products are manioc, onions and coconuts. Fishing and cattle farming are also of importance.

Lombok alternative
Long an 'add-on' destination to a Bali visit, Lombok now stands alone as an island worth several days visit. Easy international access, accommodation ranging from basic to five-star luxury, terrific snorkelling and diving, and plenty of nature and cultural attractions make Lombok well worth the visit.

People and Religion

Some 75 percent of the island's 4 million inhabitants are Sasaks, thought to have originated from the mountain tribes of northwest India or Burma. They settled on Lombok before the Malay immigrants arrived. When Islam spread from Java into the eastern regions of the Indonesian archipelago, most of the Sasaks became Muslim. The more orthodox Muslims are known as *Wetu Lima*, while another group, the *Wetu Telu*, practise a hybrid form of Islam with elements of animism and Balinese-Hinduism thrown in.

Sasak boys

Apart from the Chinese and Arabic ethnic groups, the Balinese minority accounts for the remaining population. The latter have retained their Hindu–Dharma faith. Their existence can be traced to the military campaigns of the Karangasem kingdom, who conquered North and West Lombok at the beginning of the 17th century. The Balinese feudal supremacy here continued until 1894, when they were defeated by the Dutch.

Getting There

Silk Air links Lombok with Singapore, while Merpati Airlines provides service to Kuala Lumpur, via Surabaya. Merpati and Air Mark have several flights each day between Denpasar and Lombok's capital city of Mataram. Garuda Indonesia links Mataram with Surabaya, Yogyakarta and Jakarta.

Comfortable and quicker alternatives to the usually overcrowded ferry from Padang Bai on Bali to Lembar on Lombok are the Mabua Express or Bounty Cruises. Mabua sails daily between Benoa in Bali (just north of Nusa Dua) and Lembar, the main port on Lombok. Bounty departs from Benoa for Nusa Lembongan, and continues onwards to the Gili Islands and Lombok's Senggigi Beach. The crossing takes about two hours and costs about US$30.

Star Attractions
- Senggigi Beach
- Gili Islands

BEACHES AND ISLANDS

★★ **Senggigi Beach**, the main tourist centre on Lombok, lies on the west coast of the island, about an hour's drive from Lembar or 30 minutes from the Selaparang Airport at Mataram. The resort has grown rapidly during the past few years and it now extends for several kilometres along a black sand beach. It offers lodgings of all kinds and makes an ideal base for exploring the island.

THE GILI ISLANDS

A major attraction for snorkelling enthusiasts are the three islands off the northwest coast of Lombok, ★★ **Gili Air**, ★★ **Gili Meno** and ★★ **Gili Trawangan**. All have magnificent beaches and coral reefs. Day trips from Senggigi are available, or boats can be chartered in the harbour of Bangsal, which lies north of Senggigi. Numerous hotels and guesthouses *(losmen)* are located on the islands, although on Gili Air and Gili Trawangan these are mostly very simple, with the recent addition of some grander hotels.

Below and bottom: trip to Gili Air Island, a paradise for snorkellers

Map on page 87

Lombok lore
Annually, up to 100,000 people gather at the Putri Nyale Festival on Mandalika Beach to commemorate the legend of Princess Putri Mandalika. Sought as the bride of every Lombok raja, local lore says when the beautiful princess could not choose between the suitors, she threw herself into the sea. When she jumped, hundreds of *nyale* sea worms floated to the surface. On the full moon in February, the ugly sea worms which return to spawn are gathered, fried and eaten by festival-goers, rather like a love potion.

SOUTHERN BEACHES

On the south coast of Lombok, accessible via Sukarara and Penujak *(see page 92)*, lies ★ **Kuta**. This quiet fishing village should not be confused with its famous counterpart of the same name on Bali. Visitors seeking relaxation, who are content with simple accommodation and restaurants, will feel at home. Novotel Lombok Coralia, the first international chain hotel in southern Lombok, is just east of Kuta on **Mandalika** beach. Other beaches of note in this area are **Mawun** and **Selong Blanak**, west of Kuta, while east of Kuta is the beautiful untouched beach of **Tanjung Aan**.

AROUND MATARAM

The capital of Lombok, **Mataram**, is the administrative centre for West Nusa Tenggara province. Together with neighbouring **Ampenan** and **Cakranegara**, Mataram forms a bustling urban area with a population of about 105,000. Ampenan is the quieter district, whilst Cakranegara is the island's main commercial centre.

Spices at Sweta market

CAKRANEGARA

Most of the interesting sights are centred in Cakranegara. Don't miss a tour of the biggest market on Lombok. In **Sweta**, on the eastern edge of Cakranegara, you will find not only vegetables, fruit and food of all kinds but also a wide variety of household goods and some craft items.

PURA MERU AND PURA MAYURA

Pura Meru lies on Jalan Selaparang, the main thoroughfare in Cakranegara. Founded in 1720, it was extensively restored in the early 1990s. The inner section of the temple, which is divided into three sections, is dominated by three imposing *meru* (pagodas). Its annual Pujawali festival, held over five days during the September or October full moon, is the biggest Balinese event in Lambok.

Puri Mayura, on the other side of the street, dates from the late 19th century. It is a pretty complex reminiscent of Bali's water palaces. In the middle of the lotus pond stands a pavilion known as the Bale Kambang which once housed the island's main court.

Star Attraction
- **Pura Narmada**

LINGSAR

Some 10km (6 miles) northeast of Cakranegara in **Lingsar** is the oldest temple on Lombok. ★ **Pura Lingsar** is a spacious complex built in 1714. It is regarded as the 'Mother Temple' and serves as a joint place of worship for Hindus, Muslims and followers of the *Wetu Telu* *(see page 88)*, the Malay-type race who have lived on Lombok for at least 2,000 years.

This is the temple where even local Chinese, Buddhists, Christians and occasionally *Wetu Lima* come to pray for prosperity, rain and fertility. In October, before the start of the monsoon, Hindus and Muslims gather here to pray specifically for a good harvest. The northernmost section of the complex, which is on a higher level than the rest, is the *pura* and is reserved for Hindus.

NARMADA AND SURANADI

★★ **Pura Narmada** water palace and temple is found at **Narmada**, some 12km (8 miles) to the east of Cakranegara. It is one of the largest and

Below and bottom: Pura Narmada water palace and temple details

Map on page 87

Lombok pottery

The women of Penujak, Banyumalek and Masbagik have been making pottery since the 16th century, with skills passed down from one generation to the next. Greyish-brown mud from local river-beds is manipulated into shape by hand, sometimes using a wooden paddle. Instead of using a potter's wheel, the women walk around the jar, especially if it's a large pot, building up and scraping the walls as they go. After drying in the heat of the sun, the earthenware is baked in pits fuelled by firewood and coconut husks, and then covered with rice straw. The resulting product takes on an attractive deep reddish hue.

Penujak pottery

best preserved complexes on the entire island. A Balinese prince built the palace in 1805 for his mistress, naming it after a sacred river in India. Some pools are available for swimming (modest suits are required), and traditional dances are held weekly in Narmada's splendid gardens.

You can also make a detour north to **Suranadi**, where you can stop over in the hotel of the same name, built by the Dutch, and which offers the chance to take a refreshing swim in the spring water pool. The town's Hindu shrine – ★**Pura Suranadi**, actually a complex of three temples – has a sacred spring-fed pool with sacred eels *(ikan belut)* swimming around. Visitors are welcome to feed them with hard-boiled eggs which are sold at nearby stands.

Southern Villages

Sukarara, some 25km (16 miles) southeast of Mataram, is the centre of the Sasak weaving trade. It is still a cottage industry, and visitors are invited to watch the women sitting at simple looms and weaving the fine cotton or silk *ikat* fabric using time-honoured methods *(see page 71)*.

★ **Penujak**, another 10km (6 miles) further south, is well known for its pottery, especially the thick-walled unvarnished pots and dishes of reddish-brown clay. The ★ **Lombok Pottery Centre** in Mataram (Jalan Sriwijaya 111A, Mataram) provides the best selection of distinctive Sasak pottery, including the products of other surrounding villages such as Banyumulek or Masbagik. The pottery trade in all three villages is sponsored by the New Zealand government, which lends technical and marketing expertise for the unique earthenware they produce.

★ **Rambitan**, a little further south, is a typical Sasak village, with stilt houses and characteristic rice barns with arched horseshoe-shaped roofs. Lombok's oldest mosque, **Mesjid Kuno**, is found here. For a small donation you will be taken on a guided tour of the village. South of Rambitan is **Sade** village, which is less authentic with its concrete footpaths and souvenir shops.

THE HIGHLANDS

It is worth finding time to drive through the pretty fields and rice terraces to the Lombok highlands. **Loyok** is a village of basket-makers, where workers can be observed making baskets and other items out of rattan and gambir grass. Another village, **Tetebatu**, enjoys an attractive location and a pleasantly cool climate as well as fine views of Gunung Rinjani, the sacred volcano. **Kotaraja**, just south of Tetebatu, produces some of the best handicrafts in Lombok.

Star Attraction
- **Gunung Rinjani**

GUNUNG RINJANI

Hardy trekkers with enough time on their hands should consider climbing ★★ **Gunung Rinjani**. Many visitors who have done so consider this to be the highlight of their stay in Lombok. However, it takes three full days to hike up to the summit and back. In addition, having reached the top of the mountain, with its beautiful caldera lake, the view is frequently shrouded by heavy clouds which sometimes take hours to clear.

The climb can be done either via the track at **Senaru** or **Sembalun Bumbug** villages, the latter being the more difficult route. Both guides and equipment can be hired at these villages. The best season to climb is during the dry period from May to November when the paths are not slippery.

Below: basket making
Bottom: Rambitan rice barn

Temples

Bali is often described as the 'Island of Ten Thousand Temples'. This is an understatement rather than an exaggeration, for in fact there are almost 20,000 of them, not counting the innumerable family temples and ancestral shrines which belong to every Balinese home. Every village community will have at least three main temples.

Within the boundaries of each village will be the Pura Puseh, the principal temple, looking towards the mountain, whilst in the heart of the village will be found the Pura Desa, the village temple. Towards the sea, outside the village limits and not far from the cremation ground, will be the Pura Dalem, the temple of the underworld. This is a place of worship dedicated to Shiva, the destroyer and renewer, and his consort Durga, the goddess of the dead.

In addition to these temples, there are also *banjar* and *subak* temples *(see page 18)*, royal temples belonging to the former realms of the princely rulers. Although the significance of each temple may vary, they all serve more or less the same religious function. Unlike the Christian traditions for instance, the Balinese do not meet in the *pura* for private prayer or take part in community religious services. Temples come to life only on certain festival days, when they are elaborately decorated to greet the gods.

TEMPLE ARCHITECTURE

The basic design of a Balinese temple always follows a set pattern. The temple complex is protected by a surrounding wall and is usually divided by three subsidiary walls into three courtyards, lying one behind the other and entered through gateways.

These gateways are always the most elaborate part of the temple as they serve as symbols of transition from one existence to the next. The temple is entered on the sea side through the split gate *(candi bentar)*, which embodies the division of the cosmos and the duality of human life.

The Split Gate

Balinese legend has it that the *candi bentar* – the split gate entrance of a temple – represents the two halves of the mythical Mount Meru, which was split by the mighty Shiva to become Gunung Agung and Gunung Batur, Bali's two primary volcanoes.

Opposite: a cremation ceremony construction
Below: Pura Dalem
Bottom: a split gate

THE OUTER COURTYARD

Behind the gate is the outer courtyard *(jaba)*. This is a place of assembly after arriving in the temple, and symbolises the earthly realm. It contains a number of *bale*, roofed, open-sided pavilions where visitors can rest, and often a wooden signal drum *(kulkul)* on a platform or banyan tree. This is also where offerings are prepared during temple festivals, and where the obligatory cockfight which marks the start of the festivities takes place.

Cockfighting, unless part of a temple ceremony, is officially banned in Bali, but a collection of motorbikes by the roadside and a group of wildly gesticulating men usually indicate that a cockfight is in progress. This popular sport has driven many families into ruin as gamblers will sometimes stake even their homes on the outcome of a fight.

Below: women preparing offerings
Bottom: Pura Taman Ayun

THE MIDDLE COURTYARD

The temple's elaborately decorated covered gate *(kori agung)* leads to the middle courtyard. This area is flanked by stone guardian figures *(raksaka)* to frighten away demons wishing to enter. As a double protection, there is often another wall *(aling aling)* behind this entrance against which any evil spirits not deterred by the *raksaka* will crash into. According to Balinese lore, spirits cannot turn corners.

The middle courtyard *(jaba tengah)*, which prepares the faithful for their entrance into the holy of holies, houses a large assembly hall and pavilions where the *gamelan* instruments and sacred objects used by the priests are stored.

THE INNER COURTYARD

The innermost gate provides access to the third courtyard *(jeroan)* which is reserved for the gods. The first thing you will notice are the pagoda-like shrines *(meru)*, symbolising the universal Mount Mahameru, the home of the gods. The importance of the god to which the shrine is dedicated determines the number of roofs *(tumpang)*; usually there is an uneven number between 3 and 11. In accordance with his rank, the 11-roofed *meru* is reserved for Shiva alone.

The most important part of the third courtyard, however, is the stone lotus throne *(padmasana)*, positioned with its back to Gunung Agung. During temple festivals, Shiva, in his form as the sun god Surya, takes up his position on the throne. Sometimes, however, Shiva is equated with the supreme deity Sanghyang Widhi Wasa. In this case the image of the latter will be found adorning the back of the throne. You will sometimes also find a triple *padmasana* for the *trisakti*, the divine trinity of Brahma, Wisnu and Shiva.

Also found in the *jeroan* is a reception pavilion for gods who have no special place of honour within the temple, as well as a *bale* where food offerings are made, and at least one closed shrine in which the most sacred temple relics such as *lontar* books, *keris* (ceremonial swords) and masks are safely kept.

Festivals and Ceremonies

The *kulkul* drum reverberates three times – the gods have arrived. To honour their presence, the villagers stage an elaborate festival in their temple, normally unused and unadorned on other days. The preparations last for several days, during which time the temples are decorated and

One God or many?
Although it may not appear to be so, the Balinese insist that their religion is monotheistic, in accordance with the Indonesian state policy of Pancasila – one of the hallmarks of which is the belief in one God. The Balinese recognise that there is only one supreme God, Sanghyang Widhi Wasa, but in fact pray to the myriad manisfestations of his being. These include the vast pantheon of Hindu gods, the Buddha, various deified ancestors as well as a wide range of elemental spirits.

Below: festival at Pura Taman Ayun
Bottom: traditional masks

Honour days
Special days honour deities who guard specific disciplines. Batari Dewi Saraswati, the goddess of learning and knowledge, is honoured with the blessing of books, and no reading or writing is done on that day. The Lord of Crops, Batara Sangkara, is honoured with offerings tied around coconut palms. On a day for prosperity, no business is conducted. Landep honours metal objects, daggers, cars and motorcycles. Domestic animals are blessed on Kandang, and instruments of art on Krulut Day.

Below: gamelan *orchestra*

the village streets bordered by bent bamboo canes *(penjor)* which symbolise the holy mountain. Men and women don their best sarongs. In the temple kitchen, men prepare the festive meal, the central dish being made from the meat of sacrificed animals. The *gamelan* orchestra plays for the entertainment of the deities, and the air is heavy with the scent of frangipani blossoms and burning incense. The dance and drama, which make up the entertainment, delight gods and man alike and continue into the early morning hours.

The Balinese love festivities of all kinds, and hardly a day goes by without a temple festival being celebrated somewhere. In view of the vast number of temples, it's not surprising that the **Odalan** festival is the one most frequently celebrated. Every 210 days according to the Balinese *pawukon* calendar, the members of a temple community, be it village, district or just a family, celebrate the anniversary of the temple's dedication.

Another festival celebrated throughout the island is **Galungan**, which recalls the victory over the despotic demon princes. Pigs are slaughtered for offerings and ritual feasting. The faithful greet the gods and sacred ancestors on earth. Ten days later, during **Kuningan**, spirits take their leave.

SAKA CALENDAR FESTIVALS

Apart from the *pawukon* calendar, the passage of time is also registered by another system, the *saka* calendar, introduced in AD78 when a famous Hindu saint arrived on Java from India. The date of the **Nyepi** festival, the Balinese New Year's celebration, is calculated by this calendar. On New Year's Eve, sumptuous offerings are presented to the powers of the underworld to lure them from their hiding places.

At night, the islanders stay awake and make as much noise as possible using every imaginable instrument, in order to chase away the demons. The next day is devoted to prayer and meditation. No one is allowed to eat or to work, and at night no lamps may be lit and no lights switched on, so that any demons which venture back will think that the island is uninhabited. Even tourists are not permitted to leave the hotel on this day, and the airport remains closed for 24 hours.

The Tourist Information Office produces a Calendar of Events listing the principal festivals *(see page 118)*.

RITES OF PASSAGE

Apart from these festivals, there are a large number of private ceremonies, the so-called rites of passage *(manusa yadnya)*, which accompany a Balinese from the cradle to the grave. During pregnancy, the first offerings are made to the unborn child. Immediately after its birth, its 'four companions' *(kanda mpat)*, comprising umbilical cord, placenta, blood and amniotic fluid, must be buried in a coconut shell in front of the house.

After 105 days another ceremony takes place during which the child is permitted to touch the ground for the first time. Up until then, the body and soul of the child is regarded as too immature and too precious to come in contact with the realm of the demons. On its first birthday, the child receives its name from the priest.

When the child enters puberty, there is a slew of ceremonies to mark this important transition. During the tooth-filing ceremony for instance, the incisors and canine teeth are filed down slightly

Below and bottom: taking part in a festival

to symbolically eliminate demonic characteristics and to temper passions. To cut down on expenses, however, this celebration is often postponed until when the children marry.

Below and bottom: the cremation ceremony

MARRIAGE

Balinese marriage customs are distinctive. While some favour the usual *modus operandi* of the man visiting the bride's family and asking permission for her hand, other favour the *ngorod*, or marriage by elopement. The couple will plan for their honeymoon and stage the abduction of the bride. For the sake of propriety, the bride's parents will raise the alarm and start a search for their daughter, who by this time is spending her honeymoon in a secret place. About a week later the young couple reappears and begs the parents for forgiveness. The marriage must occur within 42 days of the kidnapping, otherwise a substantial dowry has to be paid by the groom's parents.

DEATH

The most important festival, however, is the one which takes place after a person's death. Since death is not seen as final, but simply as a transition from one existence into another – with any luck, a better one – the cremation ceremony is a

cause for celebration. It is, however, expensive, which is why Balinese cemeteries are full of temporarily buried bodies, awaiting cremation. Mass cremations, in which a number of families share the costs, are the rule.

Once the necessary funds are available, the priest will calculate a favourable date. Orders are placed for a cremation tower and an animal-shaped sarcophagus, whose form depends on the caste of the deceased. If already buried, the body is disinterred, and the bones cleaned and arranged in the shape of a human body and draped with a white cloth. Relatives and friends arrive, and the cremation proper begins with a sumptuous feast.

Afterwards, the corpse is placed on the tower, which is then taken to the cremation site near the Pura Dalem. On the way, the tower containing the body is turned several times in order to confuse the spirit, so that under no circumstances will it find its way home. At the cremation site the bones are transferred to the sarcophagus, which is then ignited. The ashes, the impure part of the deceased, are scattered on the sea, freeing the soul for its next existence.

Beauty before age

Balinese buildings are not built to last an eternity, and art works are not created to last forever. Today, if you see concrete instead of carved stone ornaments on temples, it has more to do with cost-cutting than durability. Similarly, stone carvings, covered by green moss and lichen through age, are simply replaced without a pang of sentiment by new statues which will please the gods as much as the old ones.

Arts and Crafts

Bali is often described as an island of artists, and so it is all the more surprising to discover that the Balinese language has no term for 'artist' or 'art' as such. Until the dawn of the tourist era there were no professional artists on the island either. Most Balinese continue to earn a living as rice farmers, but in their spare time many are also dancers, *gamelan* players, woodcarvers or painters – to the delight of the gods, as all these artistic activities are primarily performed in their honour first and as marketable commodities second.

Below: a dancer's fan
Bottom: potter at work

STONEMASONRY

Rangda's long tongue or the sharp claws of Kala greet the visitor in many temples. Comical or grotesque forms are the speciality of Balinese stonemasons, whose fantasy seems to know no

European influence
Two European artists – Germany's Walter Spies (1895–1942) and Holland's Rudolf Bonnet (1895–1978) – together with Balinese prince Cokorde Sukawati, formed an artists' association, Pita Maha, in 1936. Within this group, various schools developed, including the Ubud and Batuan styles. A new generation of painters in the 1960s came from farming families and painted refreshing non-academic works under the guidance of Arie Smit (born 1916) from Holland.

Below: temple painting
Bottom: local artist

bounds. While a classical severity dominates the the carvings of the south, in the north they are typified by an almost baroque voluptuousness.

However, because the reliefs and sculptures are made of soft sandstone or volcanic tuff and weather quickly from the high humidity, only a handful of ancient monuments still demonstrate these characteristics. The only exception is in the Pejeng district *(see page 55)*.

Traditional Painting

In early times, the Balinese painted on strips of canvas to hang along the edge of temple roofs, or rectangular pieces of fabric used to decorate the palaces. The painting was the *wayang* or *kamasan* method, a style whose name derives from the fact that the figures were depicted in a two-dimensional manner and in three-quarters profile, rather like those of the *wayang* shadow drama *(see page 106)*. The themes were always drawn from mythology, and only natural colours were used.

An Artistic Revolution

Following the arrival of the Dutch, there were no more commissioned works from the princely palaces, and painting sank almost into oblivion. During the 1930s, however, an artistic revolution took place, due in no small part to the arrival of cultural refugees from Europe.

Young artists began to experiment with modern materials from the West. Fabrics and natural colours were replaced by paper and canvas, and oil and tempera paints. Pictures acquired the Western sense of perspective, and for the first time they were framed and signed, since individual works and not communal projects were being created. The subjects they portrayed were no longer purely religious, but also illustrated everyday themes and objects.

Various schools of painting evolved and took root, each with a distinctive style of its own, and soon Balinese art spread beyond the island's shores.

WOODCARVING

At one time, wooden shrines, pillars and roof supports of temples and palaces were covered with reliefs and creepers, brightly painted or covered with gold. Woodcarving was an art form that was always linked to architecture. Free-standing sculptures had little value, and were often restricted to masks, which are still created by carvers who enjoy the same status as priests because they are considered to have magical powers.

As in painting, centuries-old traditions were changed by the Europeans' arrival, under whose influence individual creative art began to develop. Not least for commercial reasons, these visiting sculptors encouraged the Balinese woodcarvers to create free-standing sculptures to appeal to tourists' tastes. Accordingly, many sculptures today are polished to a fine sheen, and subtly rather than garishly coloured. Clear lines are preferred over baroque shapes and secular motifs appear alongside figures of deities.

An infinite variety of items are offered for sale in the countless galleries in Ubud and Mas. Mass production has been introduced, resulting in mediocre works, but if you look hard enough, it is still possible to find original pieces done by master craftsmen. The craftsmanship of the items, usually carved out of tropical hardwoods, is often very good.

Below: modern carving
Bottom: Werdhi Budaya Art Centre

METALWORK

Goldsmiths and silversmiths have a long tradition in Bali. A visit to the workshops in Celuk *(see page 50)* provides an insight into the skills used to make jewellery and ornaments worn by Balinese women.

In former times the *keris*, a ceremonial sword, was a man's most valued possession. Even today, these weapons are proudly passed on from father to son. Long ago, the men who forged these swords held the same rank as priests, and worked in accordance with a set ritual accompanied by magic formulas which gave the *keris* a religious importance. Few craftsmen have retained these ancient skills, and most weapons for sale in souvenir shops today are derisively described as 'tourist daggers'.

Below: colourful batik
Bottom: weaving

FABRICS

Whereas carving, painting and metalwork are still traditionally masculine skills, fabric weaving is a woman's domain. Particularly attractive are the intricately designed *songket* fabrics, which use gold and silver threads to produce sarongs and blouses for ceremonial occasions. *Ikat* weaving is an art form throughout Indonesia, but *double ikat* is only produced in the village of Tenganan *(see page 71)*.

BATIK

Batik is not indigenous to Bali. It hails from Java, but the Balinese have adapted the technique using bright and bold designs and colours which are fashioned into sarongs, shirts, blouses and dresses. These are available in many shops around Kuta and Legian, and mostly produced according to sketches created by Western designers.

Both Balinese men and women buy *batik* in lengths and wrap it untailored around the waist as a skirt-like *kamben* for traditional occasions. Like any other fabric, *batik* can range in quality. Bali's home-produced cloth, *endek*, is created by hand on wooden looms and, when carefully tied and dyed, holds its colours and proves more long-lasting than mass-produced cloths.

Art's future

Since 1967, college students at Sekolak Tinggi Seni Indonesia, the College of Indonesian Arts in Denpasar, have studied traditional dance and music, puppetry and choreography for both classical and contemporary performing arts. Visitors are welcome to watch class sessions, with approval from the school's secretary (tel: 0361-273160).

Music

Gamelan musicians, who accompany dance and theatrical performances, form an essential part of every festival. Almost every *banjar* *(see page 18)* boasts its very own *gamelan* orchestra. The instruments are purchased jointly and are kept in the *bale gong*. Usually the orchestra consists of 30–40 men, although women's orchestras have become increasingly popular in recent times.

Gamelan *musicians*

The name of the orchestra is derived from the word *gamel*, which means 'hammer' in Javanese and indicates the importance of percussion instruments in the band. Forming the centre of any *gamelan* orchestra are the big drums *(kendang)*, which are played by the leader of the orchestra. In addition, there are glockenspiels *(gender)*, xylophones *(gambang)* and cymbals and gongs of various sizes. In some orchestras, there are also bamboo flutes *(suling)*.

The musicians do not improvise, although to the uninitiated they may appear to be doing so. The *gamelan* troupe plays from memory since the Balinese have no system of musical notation. Various moods can be expressed with the help of two scales – the five-note scale *slendro* conveys the feeling of joy, while the seven-note *pelog* scale tends to sound more melancholy.

Theatre and Dance

> **_Dalang_ power**
> A *wayang kulit* performance rests with one single man, the *dalang*. After a lengthy period of training, he becomes more than a puppeteer and enjoys the rank of a priest. He manipulates the puppets, whose shadows fall onto a lamp-lit screen, and simultaneously takes on all the speaking parts. Above all, the *dalang* must improvise and enliven comic figures with political asides or references to local gossip.

The great Hindu epics, *Ramayana* and the *Mahabharata*, which document the struggle between the forces of good and evil, pervade all Balinese thought.

The stories, with roots stretching back thousands of years, were brought to Southeast Asia along with Hinduism. In Indonesia, the *Ramayana* and the *Mahabharata* have been part of local folk tradition since the 11th century, when they were translated into the vernacular under King Airlangga. Every Balinese child knows the stories, and episodes are a perennially popular theme for many dance and theatre productions.

WAYANG KULIT

Wayang kulit, or shadow play, involves two-dimensional puppets stamped from buffalo hide (*wayang* = shadow; *kulit* = hide or leather); these dramatic performances served in pre-Hindu times as a religious ritual to establish contact with the ancestors. After the arrival of Hinduism, scenes from the *Ramayana* and *Mahabharata* provided the plot. *Wayang kulit* has been a popular art form since. It is, however, not just entertainment, nor is it just puppetry in the Western sense of the word. Rather, a magical ritual to re-establish the cosmic order and, more recently, as a means to convey social, political or educational messages.

Legong dancer

A PERVASIVE DANCE CULTURE

Balinese dances and dance dramas have become important advertisements for the 'Island of the Gods', but here – unlike elsewhere – they have not degenerated into a mere tourist spectacle. Bali's dance culture is more lively than ever, with almost every village having its own troupe of dancers and, thanks to income generated from tourism, they are now able to invest in new costumes, masks and ideas.

Authentic dance performances are usually held at some ungodly hour, and then only as part of a festival of several hours' duration. But visitors need not despair, as the so-called tourist performances offer excerpts from several dances, and are usually authentic and of a very high standard.

By no means are all Balinese dances old. Some drama themes date from pre-Hindu times, but many of the most famous ones were invented during the 19th century. New choreography is constantly being created by both local and foreign dance artistes.

The roots of Balinese dance drama lie in the Hindu-Dharma faith, and to this day there are no clearly defined boundaries between religious practice, art and entertainment. Even if the character of the various dances seems profane, they are nonetheless performed as offerings to the gods within the framework of a temple festival.

Below: portrait of a dancer
Bottom: detail of puppets

Fixed Repertoires

Dancers are almost all amateurs, albeit with years of arduous training behind them. Would-be Legong dancers, for example, start at the age of five. Generally, dancers specialise in one particular dance. Balinese dance usually revolves around a fixed repertoire of highly stylized and complex movements, based on the dance tradition of India. Only the comic characters have a certain amount of freedom to improvise.

BARONG

This dance, highly popular with tourists, is an exorcist ritual dating from animist times. It is performed in villages in times of crisis today, with the aim of driving out demons.

The theme of the Barong dance is the ancient struggle between good and evil in the form of two mythological creatures. Barong, representing the power of good, is portrayed by two men who wear lion's masks. The opponent is the wicked witch Rangda. The story, based on the Indian epics, leads up to a dramatic duel.

During the fight, Rangda puts a spell on the *keris* dancers who come to assist the Barong, making them turn their swords on themselves. In an authentic performance, the *keris* dancers enter a trance state. However, Barong's magic powers make the men invulnerable, so that no blood is shed. The battle finally ends in a draw, for in the Balinese cosmos good and evil belong together like day and night.

Below: Barong dance
Bottom: Kecak dancers

KECAK

The chanting of a choir of 100 men in black and white checked sarongs, a monotonous *ke-cak-ke-cak*, sends cold shivers down the spines of most spectators. The men form a circle which serves as the dance arena. Against the light of oil lamps,

the dancers relate the story of Rama and Sita. The archaic effect belies the fact that the Kecak is one of Bali's recent dance forms. The choreography was the work of Walter Spies in the 1920s, when he was searching for a dance interlude for the film *Island of the Demons*. He adapted the male choir (which here replaces the *gamelan* orchestra) from an ancient incantation ritual and combined it with scenes from the *Ramayana*. The result is one of the most impressive dances on the island.

Following the Kecak, some groups perform the **Fire Dance**, during which a man dances, while in a trance, across glowing coconut shells.

Dance delights

Joged Bumbung is one of Bali's few social dances. By means of a fan, a young dancer lures young men to join her in dance. In contrast, the Ramayana Ballet is a grand spectacle for one to sit back and enjoy. It is a colourful and fascinating depiction of the Hindu *Ramayana* epic, and takes about 90 minutes to complete.

OTHER DANCES

Almost every young Balinese girl dreams of becoming a **Legong** dancer. The Legong dancer's career begins at an early age, and it comes to an early end with the onset of puberty and its associated loss of purity. In the case of tourist performances, these rules are not always strictly observed, however.

The dance came about in the 19th century at the princely courts. It tells the story of a princess who loses her way, finds refuge at the court of a king, and then resists his approaches. The Legong is usually presented as part of a mixed programme of other dances.

The selection almost always includes **Baris**, a dance performed by men and exalting the virtues of Balinese warriors. **Kebyar Duduk** is of modern origins and describes the problems of adolescents. Its complicated movements are performed while seated and follow the choreography established during the 1920s by the famous dancer Mario (I Ketut Maria).

The **Oleg Tambulilingan** or 'Dance of the Bumble Bee' tells of the courting ritual of a pair of bumble bees and is a recent invention. The final number in an evening of dance is often the **Topeng**, a masked dance. There are a large number of masks, but a universal favourite is that of the *orang tua*, the old man whose awkward movements are parodied with gentle irony.

Topeng, a masked dance

FOOD AND DRINK

A short stroll through the night market of Denpasar or Singaraja will provide a sensory introduction to the delights of Balinese cuisine. At one corner, the aroma of freshly grilled satay will come wafting across, while at the next you will be assailed by the overpowering scent of *durian*. Everywhere the air is heavy with the sweet and spicy aroma of *kretek*, the ever popular Indonesian clove cigarettes.

With the major tourist centres offering a range of international restaurants – Italian pastas and Mexican fajitas are all the more tempting in such an exotic setting – and mobile street-side *warung* serving delicious local food, it is not too difficult to find a convenient alternative to the standard Western fare served at hotels.

LOCAL CUISINE

The basis of every Indonesian or Balinese meal is rice. So central is it to daily life that the Indonesian language distinguishes four different words for *rice*. As far as food is concerned, the most important one you should know is *nasi*, or rice as it appears on the plate. It may appear as *nasi putih* (white rice) or *nasi goreng* (rice fried with vegetables, meat and/or eggs).

Balinese food is generally hot and spicy, its flavour deriving from a blend of fresh spices, garlic, turmeric, onions and fiery chillies. Fresh coconut, either grated or squeezed for milk, adds richness and tones down the fieriness of the food, while fragrant roots and leaves give each dish its characteristic full-bodied aroma. To cater to unaccustomed Western palates, cooks in restaurants generally go easy with the chillies and spices.

Perennial favourites include *soto ayam* (chicken soup), *gado-gado* (blanched vegetables with peanut sauce) and satay (skewers of meat prepared on a charcoal grill and served with peanut sauce). These specialities are all popular in Indonesia. A number of milder dishes have been borrowed from Chinese cuisine and are recommended for those with delicate stomachs: *cap cai* is a mixed vegetable dish and *mie goreng* is fried noodles. A side dish of *sambal*, made with red-hot chillies and shrimp paste, normally accompanies a meal and should be approached with caution.

The sway-back pig is a native of Bali, and pork in general is popular on the island – unlike the rest of the country, where the majority of the population is Muslim. *Babi guling* (roast suckling pig) is often served at banquets, as is *bebek betutu* (duck roasted in banana leaves). Along the coast, excellent seafood dishes are available.

Eating Asian-style

Rice is traditionally eaten with the right hand, although in modern Balinese homes and restaurants these days, it is eaten with a spoon grasped in the right hand and a fork in the left hand – the fork is used to shovel the food onto the spoon.

When ordering rice and a variety of accompanying dishes, remember that all the food is served at the same time as they are meant to be eaten together. Diners help themselves to a serving of steaming white rice, and then to a little of each of the three or four dishes of meat or vegetables which are placed at the centre of the table for all to share.

Do not swamp your plate with food at the beginning, but keep helping yourself to a little more of the food as the meal progresses. *Nasi goreng* or *mie goreng* however, are one-dish meals and are usually eaten on their own.

Drinks and Desserts

The Balinese drink water or hot tea with their meals. During the day in the tropical climate, these are often a better choice than the admittedly light local beer. Beer fans, however, are in no danger of dying of thirst on Bali, and wine drinkers can often choose between locally produced Hatten and Indico or Wine of the Gods.

Trendy Kuta bars serve margaritas, but you could try instead *brem* (rice wine) as an aperitif or *arak* (rice liqueur) as a digestif. On a hot day, the juice of a fresh green coconut is invigorating: as well as helping to settle an upset stomach, it is an excellent thirst-quencher.

The best dessert is a plate of tropical fruits. Apart from the more familiar fruits like bananas, pineapple, papaya, mangoes and passion fruit, there are such exotic delights as *salak* (snakeskin fruit), rambutan, jackfruit and mangosteen. To round off your meal with something heavier, order black rice pudding with coconut milk *(bubur ijen)* or fried bananas *(pisang goreng)*. *Selamat makan* – bon appetit!

Restaurants

The following selections for the major tourist centres are listed according to three categories: **$$$** = expensive; **$$** = moderate; **$** = inexpensive.

Candidasa (area code 0363)

Restaurants are along the main road.
Kedai, tel: 42020. A trendy restaurant serving vegetarian and local food. **$$.**

The *durian*
An unforgettable experience is the infamous fruit known as *durian*, which is said to stink like hell and taste like heaven. Try it at least once. Descriptions of the flavour range from strawberries and cream to overripe goats' cheese.

Kubu Bali, tel: 41256. On the north end; serves the best and cheapest seafood from an open kitchen grill. **$.**
Watergarden, tel: 41540. Provides Mexican and international fare. **$$.**

Denpasar (area code 0361)

Hong Kong, Jalan Gajah Mada 99, tel: 434845. Good value Chinese food. **$.**
Kalasan Baru, Jalan Gatot Subroto, tel: 433373. Tasty local food. Try the grilled chicken and *sayur lalap* (raw vegetables in chilli sauce). **$.**
Rumah Makan Betty, Jalan Sumatra 56, tel: 224502. Delicious Indonesian food served in clean surroundings. **$.**

Kuta/Legian (area code 0361)

Aromas of Bali, Jalan Legian, Kuta, tel: 757404. Chic café-restaurant with an excellent menu for vegetarians. **$$.**
Goa 2001, Jalan Seminyak, Legian, tel: 731178. Popular nightspot and fashionable meeting place; the adjoining restaurant serves Indian and seafood. **$$.**
Kafé Warisan, Jalan Kerobokan Banjar Taman, tel: 731175. Innovative French cuisine in a garden setting. Reservations essential. **$$$.**
Ku De Ta, Jalan Laksmana, Petitengget, tel: 736969. Trendy international restaurant with wine and cigar bars. Reservations essential. **$$$.**
Made's Warung, Jalan Pantai Kuta, Kuta, tel: 755297. **Made's Warung II**, Jalan Raya Seminyak, Seminyak, tel: 732130. Perennial favourites, serving a range of Indonesian and Western dishes. **$$.**
La Lucciola, Jalan Laksmana, Petitengget, tel: 261047. Excellent Italian and Mediterranean fare by the beach. Reservations essential. **$$.**
Poppies, Gang Poppies I, Kuta, tel: 751059. The garden restaurant has an extensive menu of Western and local dishes. It is recommended you make a reservation. **$$.**

Lovina Beach (area code 0362)

Biyu Nasak, Lovina Beach, tel: 41176. Nouvelle cuisine, Bali-style. $$.

Khi Khi Seafood Restaurant, Kalibukbuk, tel: 41548. Try the grilled fish with spicy *sambal* sauce. $.

Nusa Dua (area code 0361)

Pantai Ming Garden, Jalan Pratama 216, tel: 773812. Delicious Chinese cuisine. $$.

Rai Seafood Restaurant, Jalan Pratama, Tanjung Benoa, tel: 771277. Good fish and seafood. $$.

Sendok Bar & Restaurant, Jalan Raya Nusa Dua, Galeria Nusa Dua, tel: 772850. Within walking distance of major Nusa Dua hotels. Serves excellent Indonesian food with Swiss and German specialities. $$.

Sanur (area code 0361)

Kafé Wayang, Jalan Bypass, tel: 287591. Popular with locals; serves Mediterranean-style fare and has great pastry and salad bars. $$.

Sanur Deli, Jalan Danau Poso 52, tel: 288624. Classic deli fare to take away or eat in. $$.

Spago, Jalan Danau Tamblingan 79, tel: 2882697. Pastas and salads. $$.

Swastika Restaurant, Jalan Danau Tamblingan 46, tel: 288373. Indonesian and Western food, with Balinese dances several nights weekly. $.

Trattoria Da Marco, off the Sanur Beach Hotel road, tel: 288996. Good Italian pastas and pizza. $$.

Ubud (area code 0361)

Ary's Warung, Jalan Ubud Raya, tel: 975053. A classic; good vegetarian, Balinese and Western dishes. $$.

Bebek, Jalan Hanoman, diagonally opposite the Dewi Sri Bungalows, tel: 975488. A fashionable eating place with Balinese flair. $$$.

Café Wayan, Monkey Forest Road, tel: 975447. Interesting East-meets-West cuisine and a great selection of cakes. A must-try when in Ubud. $$.

Casa Luna, Jalan Raya Ubud, tel: 973283. Diagonally opposite the Lotus Café; a meeting place for the expat community in Ubud. Cosmopolitan menu and nouvelle cuisine. $$$.

Lotus Café, Jalan Raya, tel: 975660. Popular restaurant in the centre of town, with an enchanting lotus pond as a backdrop. The specialities range from Indonesian dishes to Italian nouvelle cuisine. $$.

Murni's Warung, Campuhan, by the bridge, tel: 975233. A legend on the culinary horizon of Ubud. $$.

LOMBOK

Senggigi (area code 0370)

Asmara Restaurant, Jalan Raya Senggigi, tel: 693114. A snack bar. $$.

Café Wayan, Jalan Raya Senggigi, tel: 693098. Branch of famous counterpart in Ubud, but not as good. $$.

Sunshine Restaurant, Jalan Raya Senggigi, tel: 693232. Excellent Indonesian cuisine; good seafood. $$.

Tropicana Pub & Restaurant, Jalan Raya Senggigi, tel: 693432. A locals' gathering place for both dancing and dining. $$.

Nightlife options

Nightlife in Bali is mainly concentrated in the Kuta/Legian area. Many of the discos and clubs in the area change hands frequently and new ones open all the time. They mainly cater to young holiday-makers from Jakarta, Westerners (mainly Australians) and Japanese. Gado Gado, Peanuts and Sari Club in Kuta are perennial favourites. Double Six at Seminyak is always popular and even has a bungee-jumping operation. New on the scene at Seminyak is The Club at the Villas.

Most of the above places don't get going until midnight, and continue till past 3am.

ACTIVE HOLIDAYS

BALI BARAT NATIONAL PARK

The park administrative office (open Mon–Thur 7am–2pm, Fri 7–11am, Sat 7am–12.30pm, tel: 0365-61060) is located near Gillimanuk, the port of embarkation for ferries to Java. The office can issue entry permits and allocate guides for day trips into the western part of the park, including the offshore island of Menjangan, famous for its coral gardens *(see page 78)*. Simple accommodation is available in the park. Those wishing to camp must be accompanied by a guide and should bring tents, sleeping bags and food

COOKING

Indonesian cookery courses are held in Casa Luna restaurant in the centre of Ubud, tel: 0361-976283, and at Bumbu Bali Restaurant, Jalan Pratama, Tanjung Benoa, tel: 0361-774502, www.balifood.com Many big hotels also run cooking classes.

CRUISING

The options are many, from luxury catamarans to no-frills ketches. Try the *Wakalouka* (tel: 0361-484085, e-mail: sales@wakaexperience.com, www.wakaexperience.com), a sleek catamaran for cruises to Nusa Lembongan. The day cruise includes meals, drinks and hotel transfers. Another option is the *Bali Hai* (tel: 0361-720331, e-mail: balihai@indosat.net.id, www.balihaicruises.com), a motorised catamaran offering day cruises to Nusa Lembongan.

A similar day cruise is offered, plus a sunset dinner, aboard the *Adelaar*, a renovated 1902 Dutch clipper (tel/fax: 723604, e-mail: adelaar@indo.net.id, www.adelaar-cruises.com). If crowds aren't your scene, try the Traditional Fleet (www.songlinecruises.com) which offers private (and more expensive) cruises on board a variety of vessels.

Outrigger sailing

Colourful *jukung*, local outrigger sailboats made from hollow logs with carved bows to resemble crocodiles, are available for charter all along Sanur, Lovina and Kusamba beaches.

CYCLING

Many hotels offer bicycles or even mountain bikes for hire. Organised tours are available through Sobek or Bali Adventure Tours (see 'Rafting' for addresses).

DANCING AND MUSIC

Courses in *gamelan* playing and traditional dance are available. Check with the Ganesha Bookshop on Jalan Raya in Ubud, tel: 0361-976339.

DIVING AND SNORKELLING

The reefs of Sanur, Candidasa and Lovina offer even beginners a chance to explore Bali's underwater world. Flippers and masks are available for hire in many hotels and *losmen* (guesthouses). The most spectacular diving and snorkelling area is found just off the island of Menjagan *(see page 78)*, which forms part of the Bali Barat National Park. Diving excursions and courses can be booked through many water sports firms in the tourist centres. Bali Hai Diving Adventures, Benoa Harbour, tel: 0361-724062, e-mail: diverse@indosat.net.id, www. balihaicruises.com; and Dive Indonesia, Jalan Pantai Kuta 7, Kuta, e-mail: deepblue@idola.net.id Both have a comprehensive programme of courses and diving equipment.

GOLF

The 18-hole golf course at the Bali Handara Kosaido Country Club, tel: 0362-22646, www.balihandarc.co.id, north of Lake Bratan in the cool mountains, is one of the loveliest in the world. Guest players are welcome. Another option is the 18-hole Bali Golf and Country Club at Nusa Dua, tel 0361-771791, e-mail: reservat@BaliGolfandCountryClub.com, www.BaliGolfandCountryClub.com Named Indonesia Best Golf Resort, Le Meridien Nirwana Golf & Spa Resort in Tabanan, has spectacular holes across the Indian Ocean, tel: 0362-81970, e-mail: sales@balimeridien.com, www.lemeridien-bali.com

MEDITATION

Buddhist temples in North Bali villages offer secluded and peaceful sites for meditation. Open 24-hours daily, visitors are welcome. Simple accommodation and food available. Contact Robby, tel: 081-6574434 or 6582005.

MOUNTAIN CLIMBING AND JUNGLE WALKS

Both Gunung Agung and Gunung Batur can be climbed in a day's excursion. The starting points are Besakih and Toya Bungkah respectively. You need to be fit, and good hiking boots are essential. For both trips you will need warm clothing. Take food along with you if you are climbing Gunung Agung. Mountain guides are not strictly necessary, but will make life easier. They can be hired in any one of the *losmen* at your starting point.

The trip to the top of Gunung Batur and back will take about four to five hours; Gunung Agung takes at least twice as long. To climb Gunung Rinjani on Lombok *(see page 93)* you will need approximately four days. More information can be obtained at the Senggigi beach area.

Guided walks through the jungle or rice paddies can be booked through Sobek or Bali Adventure Tours (see 'Rafting' for addresses). Try also Bali Bird Walks, Tues, Fri, Sat and Sun at 9.15am (tel: 0361-975009).

RAFTING

The latest rage amongst the adventurous is white-water rafting on the Ayung River in Kedewatan near Ubud *(see also page 35)*. Rafters can be picked up from their hotels along the south coast. The best time to go rafting is during the rainy season from November to March when the water levels are reasonably high. Information and reservations: Bali Adventure Tours, tel: 0361-721480, e-mail: info@baliadventuretours, www.baliadventuretours.com; Sobek Bali Adventure Specialists, tel: 0361-287059, e-mail: sales@sobek.co.id

SURFING

Surfboard novices hurl themselves into the waves on Kuta beach. Experts prefer the waves at Suluban, Canggu and Mendewi beaches. Surfing is reasonably good throughout the year and especially good from June to August. Surfboards can be rented inexpensively at Ulu's Shop in Jalan Bakungsari and at Amphibia Surf Shop at Jalan Legian in Kuta.

Spas and massages

Since the 1990s, Bali has become Asia's premier spa destination. Most star-rated hotels have full spa services, or at least traditional massage. Many stand-alone spa facilities such as Bodyworks offer the full range of spa treatments too. Most therapies centre around Balinese and Indonesian traditional healing remedies, originating from ancient royal palaces and practised by nearly every Indonesian in daily life.

PRACTICAL INFORMATION

Getting There

BY AIR

Ngurah Rai International Airport, 13km (8 miles) southwest of Denpasar, is served by daily flights from Jakarta, Yogyakarta, Surabaya, Makassar, Mataram and other points in Indonesia by the national airline Garuda, and smaller domestic airlines like Merpati and Bouraq. Bali is well connected with international flights from the US (Los Angeles, San Francisco and New York), Europe (London, Amsterdam, Frankfurt, Paris and Zurich), Australia (Sydney, Melbourne and Darwin), and Asia (Singapore, Kuala Lumpur, Bangkok, Tokyo and Hong Kong). Some airlines fly only as far as Jakarta, where you transfer to one of several daily flights to Bali. The Tourist Information Office has a counter at the airport where rooms can be booked, and there are bureaux de change and a taxi stand.

An airport tax of 75,000 Rp is charged on leaving the country, 11,000 Rp for domestic flights. Most airlines require confirmation of flight reservations at least 72 hours prior to departure. Ask for the re-confirmation code.

BY BUS

Considerably more tiring is the overnight trip by air-conditioned express bus from Denpasar to Surabaya or on to Yogya or Jakarta. As it takes about 24 hours to get to Denpasar, the bus is best for the truly adventurous. There are also bus connections to other cities in Java. The ferry portion of the journey (the boat arrives at Gilimanuk on the western coast of Bali) is included in the price of the bus ticket. Some buses go directly to Kuta or Sanur, but most end up at Denpasar. In Bali, bus companies have their offices at Jalan Diponegero and Jalan Hasannudin in Denpasar.

BY TRAIN

Trains are slower but ideal if you have the time. From Jakarta, take the train to Banyuwangi on Java's eastern tip, where you catch the bus that takes you to Bali by ferry.

BY SEA

If travelling overland from Java, the ferry leaves Ketapang for Gilimanuk on the western coast of Bali, the trip taking about 30 minutes. From Lembar, Lombok, ferries run regularly to Padang Bai, near Candidasa in eastern Bali or Benoa Harbour in Southern Bali. An express catamaran service also plies between Lembar and Benoa in southeast Bali. For further information, see page 88. Padang Bai is visited twice every month by the passenger ship *Kelimutu*, run by the state-owned shipping line Pelni. The ship covers a two-week circuit around established routes in the Indonesian archipelago. The Pelni office can be contacted at Benoa, tel: 0361-720962.

Once weekly, a fast ferry departs from Benoa Harbour for Bima (Sumbawa) and Kupang (West Timor). Contact Gama Dewata Bali Tours, tel: 0361-263568 or 232704

Getting Around

FROM THE AIRPORT

Taxis are available at the taxi counter, and rates are posted for trips to the various centres in cars with air-conditioning. The fare is paid at the counter. Refuse offers from touts and informal guides loitering at the airport. Major hotels and pre-arranged tours provide their own transport.

BY BUS AND *BEMO*

Public buses are cheap, if uncomfortable, with routes that do not pass through the main tourist centres. Much more efficient is the shuttle bus run by the Perama Tourist Service. These run several times a day on the main routes between the tourist centres. Tickets can be bought in many *losmen* (guesthouses) and at travel agents in the main tourist areas.

Even cheaper is the *bemo*, a covered pick-up, which usually runs along a prearranged route but which has no set bus stops. To get out, make your presence known by calling out to the driver. To check on the fare, ask the other passengers and pay the conductor the correct sum – otherwise, as a foreigner, you are likely to pay over the odds. In tourist centres, public *bemos* can be chartered for the day or for a one-way trip to a specific destination.

DOKAR

In Denpasar, Singaraja and Klungkung there are still horse-drawn carriages *(dokar)* for hire. *Dokar* have also put in an appearance in Kuta, where they are a tourist attraction.

TAXIS

Metered taxis are available in the tourist centres along the south coast or can be booked by phone. Elsewhere, a taxi – usually a minibus – is simply a hired car with driver, or a chartered *bemo*. They are usually rented for day trips. The price depends on the distance travelled but expect to pay about Rp10,000 for the hour and Rp100,000 for the day.

CARS AND MINIBUSES

The international car rental firms have branches at some of the luxury hotels along the south coast. Local firms are plentiful and significantly cheaper. An international driving licence or local tourist license is legally required, but generally overlooked if a valid foreign driving license is available. The vehicles are usually Suzuki jeeps or the larger Toyota Kijang.

Depending on its condition, the rental period and the negotiating skills of the hirer, a jeep will cost Rp75,000–125,000 a day from a local firm. In addition, there are insurance charges. Before signing a rental agreement, take a test drive to check on the condition of the vehicle, especially the brakes and air-conditioning.

As you step out of your hotel, you will be deluged with offers of "transport" for car and minibus rental. The following companies can be recommended (all numbers area code 0361):

Avis, Jalan Uluwatu 8A, Jimbaran, tel: 701770.

Toyota Rent-a-Car, Jalan Raya Tuban 99X, tel: 751282.

Bagus Car Rental, Jalan Duyung 1, tel: 287794.

Mega Jaya, Jalan Raya Tuban 78X, tel: 753760.

CV Garlic, Jalan Raya Legian Utara, Legian, tel: 730491, 730196.

Nusa Dua Rent-a-Car, Jalan Pantai Mengiat, Nusa Dua, tel: 771905.

Drive crazy

In general, a rented car without a driver is recommended only for experienced drivers. The Indonesians drive on the left-hand side, but the crucial (unwritten) rule of the road is that the stronger or larger always has right of way. Drivers appear to resemble kamikaze pilots, which seems out of character given the gentle Balinese temperament. Chickens and dogs are active participants in the traffic mêlée and should be mercilessly hooted off the road. If you don't feel up to facing such traffic on holiday, pay a little more and negotiate for a car with a driver. If there are enough of you, rent a minibus with a driver.

Motorcycles

Rental agencies are found at all the tourist centres. Although this is an economical way of travelling – expect to pay about Rp35,000–50,000 a day – the chance of a traffic accident significantly increases. Crash helmets are compulsory and must be provided by the rental firm. Although the feeling of freedom that comes from riding a motorbike while wearing a minimum of clothing is tempting, your skin will be the first to suffer if you have an accident on any of the island's roads.

In the south there are plenty of fuel stations run by the state-owned oil company Pertamina. In more remote areas, look for the sign 'Premium' at roadside kiosks. Try to avoid village kiosks with handpainted signs, as the quality of the fuel sold by these is of dubious quality.

Facts for the Visitor

Travel Documents

To enter Indonesia, visitors from almost 50 countries require only a return air ticket and a passport valid for at least six months from the planned date of departure.

A two-month entry permit is granted automatically on arrival but this can't be extended, although if you leave the country you are allowed to re-enter again, even the same day, for another two months.

Visitors from all other countries must obtain a one-month visa from their local Indonesian embassy or consulate. Business travellers intending to work in Bali require a business visa in advance of arrival.

Customs

Items for personal use, including film and video cameras, typewriters and binoculars, may be imported freely. Other allowances include 2 litres of alcoholic drinks, 200 cigarettes (50 cigars or 100g tobacco), a reasonable amount of perfume, and presents to a total value of US$250. There is a ban on the import of Chinese medicines, pornographic materials, pre-recorded video cassettes, weapons, narcotics and fresh fruit.

Items more than 50 years old are classified as 'national treasures' and subject to export restrictions. Items which contravene the Convention of International Trade in Endangered Species will be confiscated and smugglers prosecuted.

Tourist Information

The local Tourist Information Office in Bali will supply information free of charge. Don't forget to ask for the Calendar of Events listing the main festivals. Information offices usually open Mon–Thur 8am–2pm, Fri 8am–11am and Sat 8am–12.30pm.

Denpasar: Badung Government Tourist Office, Jalan Kuta Raya 2, Kuta, tel: 0361-756175; Bali Government Tourist Office, Jalan Supratman, Niti Mandala, Renon, tel: 0361-754090.

Ubud: Bina Wisata Tourist Centre, Jalan Raya Ubud, opposite the Pura Desa in the centre of town. Also sells tickets for dance performances and has up-to-the minute information e.g. concerning temple festivals (8am–9pm, tel: 0361-973285).

Lombok: Department of Tourism, Art & Culture, (Regional Office, West Nusa Tenggara) Jalan Singosari 2, Mataram, tel: 0370-634800, 632723, 635308, 635874, fax: 637233; Lombok-Sumbawa Tourism Promotion Board, Lombok Raya Hotel, Jalan Panca Usaha 11, Mataram, tel: 0370-641220, fax: 634224, email: visitlombok@mataram.wasantara.net.id, www.visitlombok.com

CURRENCY AND EXCHANGE

The Indonesian unit of currency is the Rupiah (Rp) and is available in notes of 100, 500, 1,000, 5,000, 10,000, 20,000, 50,000 and 100,000. Coins are found in 25, 50, 100, 500 and 1,000 denominations. It is wise to carry smaller notes especially in the remote areas, as vendors may not carry enough change to break larger notes. The import and export of local currency is limited to Rp50 million. There are no restrictions concerning the import and export of foreign currency.

Money can be changed at banks and at licensed bureaux de change in the major tourist centres. The latter are open every day until late at night. Try to avoid changing money in hotels as the exchange rate is not so favourable.

Visitors should bring traveller's cheques in US$. MasterCard and Visa credit cards are accepted by the larger hotels and many art galleries; American Express is less widely accepted.

TIPPING

Tipping is alien to Indonesian culture, but this is slowly changing as a result of increased tourism. Today, waiters in top hotels and restaurants expect a small tip, even if a service charge has already been added to the bill. Porters expect at least Rp1,000 per item of luggage. Chambermaids and taxi drivers, too, will be pleased to receive a small tip.

SHOPPING

It is not easy to curb one's enthusiasm for shopping in Bali. In Mas you will be tempted by woodcarvings, in Celuk by silverware, in Ubud by the famous paintings, and in Tenganan by fabrics and items made from lontar leaves. Cheap tropical clothes can be bought everywhere, and the souvenir stands in the tourist centres are piled high with crafts of all kinds.

In the tourist centres, you will often be approached by traders of every kind. Attempt to affect disinterest and try, above all, to remain friendly, even if it is difficult to do so. Remember that the salesmen are just trying to earn a living. Bargaining is the norm in markets, smaller shops and art galleries, although it is considered good manners not to fight for the last penny. Increasing numbers of boutiques are adopting a fixed-price policy.

When buying souvenirs, check on export regulations. Any item which is over 50 years old is classified as an antique and its export is restricted. It is prudent to remember that the Washington Agreement prohibits the import of certain goods, e.g. those made with ivory, tortoiseshell and snakeskin, into Europe and the US. Other countries, such as Australia, have restrictions on animal, sea or agricultural products.

Driving a bargain

In shops without a 'fixed price' policy, bargaining is the norm. Start at one-third of the asking price, and the vendor will start lowering his or her price as you raise yours. Stop at the amount that you really want to spend – about half to two-thirds of the asking price. If the seller refuses, just walk away; you'll probably be called back to buy at your last bid. If so, you are morally obliged to buy the item at the agreed price. While bargaining can be a fun experience, don't go overboard with honing your skills, especially at villages. The extra dollar that you paid will go to feed a hungry mouth or two.

OPENING TIMES

Banks: Monday to Friday 8am–2pm.

Shops: most are open daily until 9pm or 10pm.

Government offices: Monday to Thursday 7am–3pm, Friday 7.30am–noon.

PUBLIC HOLIDAYS

Official holidays: 1 January (New Year); April (Good Friday/Easter); May (Buddhist Waisak); 17 August (Independence Day); 25 December (Christmas).

Other official holidays with dates that change with the lunar calendar include: Chinese New Year; Balinese New Year (Nyepi, Day of Silence); Muslim Idul Fitri, Mohammad's Birthday and Idul Adah.

The various religious festivals are too numerous to list. Their dates vary from year to year as they are calculated according to the *Lunar Pawukon* or *Saka* calendars. The Tourist Information Office produces a *Calendar of Events* which lists the various dates for the coming year.

Note: Nguran Rai International Airport is closed for 24 hours on the Balinese New Year, Nyepi.

POSTAL SERVICES

Post offices *(Kanto Pos dan Giro)* in Denpasar and major towns are usually open from Monday to Thursday 8am–2pm, on Friday 8am–noon and on Saturday 8am–1pm. Stamps can also be bought from the postal services counters in the tourist centres and in many hotels. Mail to Europe and the US takes about 10 days, air parcels take between two to three weeks, sea parcels about three months. There are numerous reliable cargo companies that can ship your shopping home in the various tourist centres. Denpasar's Central Post Office is open 7.30am–8.30pm daily, 8am–8pm, Sundays.

TELEPHONES

The Indonesian telephone network is hopelessly overloaded. If you plan to use a public call box you will need a great deal of patience and a large supply of 100 Rp coins. Card telephones are becoming more frequent.

International direct dialling is available at telecommunications offices *(Wartel)* at the major tourist centres, and of course from hotels, although the charges levied by the latter are frequently very high. Many hotels have card telephones and provide the phone cards at reception. For international calls, dial 001 or 008, then the country code followed by the number itself.

The access codes for US phone cards are as follows: MCI: 00180111; Sprint: 00180115; AT&T: 00180110.

The country code for Indonesia is 62. Bali area codes are as follows: Denpasar, Ubud, Kuta, Nusa Dua, Sanur and Jimbaran – 0361; Singaraja – 0362; Amlapura – 0363; Negara – 0365; Bangli and Klungkung – 0366; Bedugul – 0368.

TIME

There are three time zones in Indonesia. Bali and Lombok both use Central Indonesian Time, which is GMT + 8 hours. Indonesia does not use Daylight Savings Time.

ELECTRICITY

The voltage in Indonesia is generally 220V. Although adapters are available for loan in the better hotels, it is advisable to bring the appropriate one along with you, i.e. two round prongs.

MEDICAL

The only vaccination required by law is that against yellow fever for visitors arriving from an infected area. Officially, Bali is malaria-free. Prophylaxis is only recommended if travelling to Lombok or further eastward. Ensure that you have a valid vaccination against polio and tetanus. Also recommended are vaccinations for hepatitis A and B protection.

The usual over the counter medicines are available in pharmacies *(apotik)*. They are generally inexpensive and available without prescription. You should, however, take a supply of frequently needed items with you. Preparations for the treatment of diarrhoea, sunburn and colds should be included. Local preparations are often the most effective against insect bites (ask in your hotel or an *apotik*).

You should observe certain basic health rules in order to minimise the risk of infection. Allow yourself enough time to acclimatise and do not underestimate the strength of the sun's rays. Remember to use suntan lotion (SPF 18 or more) and a sun hat. Air-conditioning is a mixed blessing due to the abrupt change from heat outside to fridge-like temperatures indoors. In most cases, fans are preferable and provide sufficient relief.

Outside the major hotels you should eat only cooked or fried foods. Avoid tap water, salads, and unpeeled fruits. Bottled mineral water is widely available, and some hotels also supply flasks of purified water for drinking in the rooms. Experienced travellers in the tropics never touch alcohol before sundown. Trying Balinese food is an essential part of the holiday experience and, as long as you observe the basic precautions, you should enjoy it.

EMERGENCIES

Medical care in Indonesia is not up to Western standards yet. A private health insurance policy, including emergency transport back home if necessary, is strongly advisable.

For minor ailments, go to Bali International Medical Centre, Jalan Bypass Ngurah Rai 100X, Simpang Siur, Kuta, tel: 761263. This private clinic specialises in the treatment of foreign tourists and has advanced life support ambulances and air evacuation services.

Emergency dental treatment can be obtained from Dr Retno Agung, Jalan Bypass Ngurah Rai, Sanur, tel: 288501. In the case of serious illness, it is strongly recommended that you fly to Singapore or Australia.

CLOTHING

Light cotton clothing is ideal for Bali's warm, humid tropical climate. Don't pack too many clothes, as you won't be able to resist the items on sale throughout the island. If you plan excursions into mountainous regions, a warm pullover is useful. A sun hat and an umbrella are useful accessories and can be purchased locally.

ETIQUETTE

Signs at temple entrances often indicate the type of clothing considered appropriate. No one may enter a temple without a waist sash. Buy one at the start of the visit and carry it with you if you plan to visit other temples, otherwise sarongs and sashes are usually available for rent at the entrances. Since blood defiles a temple, people with bleeding wounds and menstruating women may not enter. Their presence would necessitate a purification ceremony.

During ceremonies, *pakaian adat* clothing is desirable. This is the traditional festive clothing prescribed by the *adat*, the unwritten law, of the Balinese. When in doubt at temple ceremonies, do as the Balinese themselves do – kneel when they do so, and make sure at all times that your head is not higher than that of the priest.

Festival clothing

If you plan to visit a temple during a major festival, it is mandatory that you are dressed in *pakaian adat*, or customary festival clothing. This means donning a long hip cloth, sash and sleeved shirt, with men wearing a folded headcloth and short overskirt over their long trousers as well.

Nudity on the beach is impolite and illegal. Wear your bathing suit at the beach or the pool.

The head is considered holy, and even lovingly stroking a child's hair is regarded as an insult to dignity. Correspondingly low in the hierarchy come the feet, which should never be pointed or even directed at anyone. Similarly taboo is the left hand: remember to use your right for giving and receiving things. The exchange of affection in public is not acceptable, and in temples it is forbidden. Begging is generally frowned upon, and you are advised not to give anything to begging children.

In an argument, avoid gesticulating wildly and making a scene – when in doubt, a smile can help to bridge linguistic and cultural barriers.

Photography

Film can be readily purchased in Bali, although it is not always stored under ideal conditions.

Take plenty of films with you, as Bali offers a wealth of photographic opportunities. Do not forget that the locals are not automatically suitable subjects. Exercise discretion and ask for permission before photographing individuals, especially during religious festivals. Sign language is usually adequate. The use of flash is forbidden during night ceremonies in temples.

Theft

Petty theft is becoming increasingly commonplace in Bali's tourist centres. Leave expensive jewellery at home and keep valuables in the hotel safe.

Diplomatic Representation

Australia, Canada: Jalan Prof. Moch Yamin 51, Renon, Denpasar, tel: 235092, 235093, fax: 235146.
Britain: Jalan Mertasari 2, Sanur, Denpasar 80227, tel: 270601, fax: 270570.
France: Smailing Tours, Jalan Bypass Ngurah Rai 88X, Sanur, tel: 288224.
Germany: Jalan Pantai Karang No 17A, Sanur, tel: 288535, tel/fax: 288826.
Italy: Lotus Enterprises, Jalan Bypass Ngurah Rai, Jimbaran, tel: 701005.
Netherlands: KCB Travel, Jalan Raya Kuta 127, Kuta, tel: 751517, fax: 752777.
Sweden & Finland: Jalan Segara Ayu, tel: 288407, fax: 287242.
Switzerland & Austria: c/o Swiss Restaurant, Jalan Werkudaya (Jalan Rum Jungle) Legian Kelod, tel: 751735, fax: 754457.
United States: Jalan Hayam Wuruk 188, Renon, tel: 233605.

Glossary

Adat: Unwritten law based on tradition
Bale: Open pavilion in the courtyard of a temple
Banjar: District of a Balinese village which includes the married male members of the community
Meru: Shrine with multiple roofs derived from Mount Mahameru, the sacred mountain of Hinduism
Odalan: Festival marking the anniversary of the dedication of a temple
Pura: Temple
Puri: Palace
Tirtha: Holy water
Trimurti: The Hindu trinity of Brahma, Shiva and Vishnu

Showing respect

The Balinese, and in fact Indonesians in general, always show great respect when addressing others, especially when a younger person speaks to his or her elders. The custom is to address an older man as *bapak* or *pak* (father) and an older woman as *ibu* (mother). The same terms are often used to address younger people too, if they are deemed worthy of respect.

ACCOMMODATION

If you want to enjoy unadulterated luxury in a Balinese setting, expect to spend at least US$250 or more a night. At posh retreats like the Aman resorts – of which there are three in Bali – rooms cost at least double that. The good news, however, is that there is no need to sleep on the beach if you can't afford to fork out such huge sums. Clean and comfortable rooms can be had for much less.

After the 10-storey Bali Beach Hotel at Sanur was built in the 1960s, a regulation was passed prohibiting the construction of buildings taller than palm trees. Architects also began to add local flavour to hotels by making use of local building techniques and materials. In many instances, tropical vegetation has helped to turn hotel complexes on Bali into miniature paradises.

There is a wide choice of accommodation on Bali. If you aren't too demanding, you will immediately feel at home in a *losmen*, a small guesthouse with simple rooms. These are generally run by Balinese families, and offer the chance to establish contact with the local people. Around Ubud, many families earn extra income by letting out one or more rooms in their home to tourists.

Hotels

The following are hotel recommendations for destinations covered in this book. They fall roughly into the following price categories: **$$$** = expensive; **$$** = moderate; **$** = inexpensive.

Bedugul (area code 0362)

Bali Handara Kosaido Country Club, tel: 22646, fax: 23048, e-mail: sale@balihandara.famili.com, www.balihandara.co.id **$$$**.

Candidasa (area code 0363)

Amankila, tel: 41333, fax: 41555, e-mail: amankila@idola.net.id, www.amanresorts.com This Aman resort is one of the nicest on the island, lying a few kilometres outside Manggis village. The multi-tiered 'infinity' pool with views of the sea is breathtaking. Rooms start at US$550. **$$$**.

Kubu Bungalows, tel: 41256, fax: 41531, e-mail: info@kububali.com, www.kububali.com Enchanting location on the mountainside; various price categories available. **$$**.

Pondok, tel: 41818. Central location on the beach. The best choice in the bottom-of-the range category. **$**.

Puri Bagus, tel: 41131, fax: 41290, e-mail: pbcandi@denpasar.wasantara.net.id, www.balimart.com/byronhotels.html Pleasant beach resort. **$$$**.

The Watergarden, e-mail: watergarden@denpasar.wasantara.net.id Exclusive little complex away from the beach. An excellent choice for visitors in search of absolute peace and attractive surroundings. **$$$**.

Candi Kuning/Bedugul (area code 0368)

Kalaspa Health Retreat, Banjar Asah Panji Ds. Wanagiri Kec. Sukasada, tel: 0316-419606, fax: 419607, e-mail: sales@kalaspa.com, www.kalaspa.com Beautiful resort overlooking Lake Tamblingan. Health programmes, villas, charming tearoom in colonial style. **$$$**.

Denpasar (area code 0361)

Natour Bali Hotel, Jalan Veteran 3, tel: 225681, fax: 235347, e-mail: ntrbali@denpasar.wasantara.net.id Tourists no longer stay in Denpasar, but this historic hotel is worth mentioning as it dates from colonial times. **$$**.

Jimbaran (area code 0361)

Bali Inter-Continental, Jalan Uluwatu, tel: 701888, fax: 701777, e-mail: bali@interconti.com, www.baliinterconti.com Set in 14 hectares (35 acres) of landscaped gardens with 425 rooms. Outstanding architecture; faces a beautful white sandy beach. **$$$.**

The Four Seasons, Jalan Uluwatu, tel: 701010, fax: 701020, e-mail: fsrb @indosat.net.id, www.fourseasons.com Built on a terraced hillside amidst beautiful gardens, this deluxe resort has 147 exquisite villas, each with a private splash pool. An ideal honeymoon getaway but expect to pay at least US$300 a night. **$$$.**

Kuta/Legian (area code 0361)

Asana Santhi Willy, Jalan Tegal Wangi 17, Kuta, tel: 752273, fax: 752641, e-mail: asanasw@indo.net.id Small, centrally located complex with comfortable rooms and a family atmosphere. Near the beach. **$.**

Barong Cottages, Jalan Segara Batu Bolong, Kuta, tel: 751804, fax: 751520, e-mail: barong66@indo.net.id, www.balihotels.com/kuta/barong.htm Small and charming complex with swimming pool. **$.**

Bintang Bali Hotel, Jalan Kartika Plaza, tel: 753292, fax: 751260, e-mail: bintang@idola.net.id Luxurious rooms and suites set in landscaped gardens with a private stretch of beach. Wide range of restaurants and facilities such as swimming pool, fitness centre, squash and tennis courts. **$$$.**

Legian Beach, Jalan Melasti, Legian, tel: 751711, fax: 752651, e-mail: legian-grup@denpasar.wasantara.net.id Pleasant hotel for groups, directly on the beach and conveniently situated between Kuta and Legian. Suitable for families; excellent cuisine. **$$.**

The Oberoi Bali, Jalan Laksmana, tel: 730361, fax: 730791, e-mail: reservation@theoberoi-bali.com, www.oberoihotels.com A luxury bungalow complex on what is probably the loveliest beach on the island. The best address in Kuta/Legian and one of the best on the island. Rooms from US$200 up. **$$$.**

Poppies Cottages, Poppies Lane, Kuta, tel: 751059, fax: 752364, e-mail: info@bali.poppies.net, www.poppies.net A classic amongst the typical local bungalow complexes; the same applies to the adjoining garden restaurant. Reservations recommended. **$$.**

Santika Beach Hotel, Jalan Kartika Plaza, tel: 751267, fax: 751260, e-mail: santika@denpasar.wasantara.net.id Situated on the outskirts of Kuta in a lovely garden. **$$.**

Lovina Beach (area code 0362)

Bali Lovina Beach Cottages, Lovina Beach, tel/fax: 41385. Modern bungalows in a pretty garden setting, with a swimming pool. **$$.**

Banyu Alit Beach Inn, Lovina Beach, tel: 41789, fax: 41563, e-mail: banyualit@iname.com, www.angelfire.com/id/banyualit Clean and well furnished rooms and bungalows, and a friendly atmosphere. The restaurant is also recommended. **$$.**

Palma Beach Hotel, Lovina Beach, tel: 41775, fax: 41659. Spacious rooms, and a welcoming atmosphere. Reservations recommended. **$$.**

Purnama Homestay, Lovina Beach, tel: 22288, fax: 21090. Comfortable accommodation and friendly staff. **$.**

Sol Inn Lovina, Lovina Beach, tel: 41265, fax: 41659, e-mail: sollovina@singaraja.wasantara.net.id The only international chain hotel operation in Lovina. **$$.**

Pemuteran (area code 0362)

Pondok Sari Beach Bungalows, tel/fax: 92337, e-mail: pdkjkt@yahoo.com Tastefully decorated bungalows in an idyllic setting. **$$.**